I AM CHAMPION:

7 *LAWS of Winning Against All Odds*

William Jennings Jr

Copyright © 2015 by William Jennings Jr

All rights reserved

Published September 2015

By CheckMyBookstore Publishing

The scanning, uploading and distribution of this book via internet or any other means without express permission of the publisher is illegal and is punishable by law. Your support of the author's rights is appreciated. For additional information or any other inquiries, please send an email to wjennings@checkmybookstore.com.

I would like to acknowledge all family members, friends, colleagues, and mentors near and far that has supported me along the way. I send out a sincere thanks to you all.

A special thanks to the editor of this book TJ Rose for help during this process if you are in need of editing services checkout www.authortjrose.com

Table of Contents

1. The Belief Effect…………………… 8

2. The Real YOU…………………….. 24

3. Taking Control……………….…... 38

4. *Pain: The Name of the Game*………….. 52

5. The Heat………………………….... 63

6. The Now Factor…………………… 71

7. Commitment……………………. 84

8. Conclusion……………………… 94

9. About Author……………………. 97

I AM CHAMPION

Introduction

When I think of a Champion, I think of someone who has faced some great obstacle and conquered it. I think of someone who, in the midst of struggle, came out on top. I am not sure I could consider someone a Champion who's had everything handed to them. If you were born into money that is okay, but in my opinion, you do not become a Champion until you go conquer something extremely difficult. I also must say that not all Champions are rich or have money. Money does not necessarily qualify you as a Champion; I believe Champions are those that came out a winner despite being in a losing situation. The dictionary defines it as *a person who has defeated or surpassed all rivals in a competition*. Well, in the competition of life, we are all fighting to be the best we can be, and to surpass anything or anyone that gets in our way! Therefore, whatever you feel is your best, keep that in mind when I refer to the term Champion, and I'm talking about your biggest/wildest dream that you have held in your heart, knowing that it could someday come into reality for you.

I wrote this book because a large portion of the population was not born into money nor given a lot of opportunities. If you are like me, when you arrived here you quickly realized that every odd was against you. No real role models, no opportunities, mis-educated, broke, and surrounded by negativity. Against these odds, most people faint. Against these kinds of odds, most people will throw in the towel. Against these odds, most people will give up on life and any dream they may have held, and I believe this is the worst thing that can happen to a person. My odds may not be the same as your odds, but I believe we all have a mountain to climb. If you would like to make it to the top of your mountain, then you have picked up the right book.

In this book, I lay out simple but power principles on how you can win against any and every obstacle that you face. I give real life examples of situations I've faced that attempted to break my spirit, take my mind, and even take my life. I believe that if I could make it out of the hellish conditions from which I came, you can too. I also give examples of people who have made it out of worse conditions than what I personally went through, and how they did it. Sometimes, we complain about what others would probably kill to have. You may have just what you need to get where you are trying to go. Champions are not only winners, but also they are fighters; they are courageous, persistent, positive, and they have the ability to influence other people. Champions don't give up easily, and Champions do not take no for an answer.

If you feel a Champion rising up out of you from the inside, you have picked up the right book. I will walk you through seven laws that I have used to achieve different levels of success, and still use each and every day in a hope that they will help guide me into greatness. I must emphasize that these are "laws," so if any one of them are broken, it is impossible for you to become a Champion. All seven must work together for you to become the Champion you know you can be. You may not do them all great, but all seven must be applied to your life in one way or another. When you break the law in society, you pay the consequences, and so it is with these laws, except the consequence you may pay is living a miserable unfulfilled life; the ultimate tragedy.

This is not a fairy-tale or a made up story. These are real life events and principles that anybody can use, no matter where you start out in life. I have studied successful people for years and have read countless books and biographies, which led me to compile a list of what they all have in common. Every principle mentioned in this book has been used in one way or another by every Champion to achieve success. I give examples of how I personally utilized the laws, but great people are using them every day, and it is why they are winning. It is time for you to go get what you know you should have and take a slice out of the winner's pie. Are you tired of just watching the game, seeing everyone else becoming winners? Are you now ready to jump in and start competing? I AM Champion: it's about game changers, move makers, barrier breakers, and the unstoppable personality. A *win by any means* mentality, a *win or else* intuition, and a *surely I deserve to be on top* mindset and focus. If this is you, then you have picked up the right book. If you are okay with keeping things in your life as is, then this may not be for you. However, if you are ready to knock down some walls, beat down some doors, surprise some friends and family, and find favor in high places, well, this is the book for you.

I am excited to get started with depositing these important laws into your life, so that you can begin to finally see the results you have been looking for. These principles work each and every time they are applied. This is not a hit or miss, nor is this about winning by chance or luck. These are proven, basic techniques that anyone can use. I must emphasize the word "basic" to show these laws are not complicated whatsoever. They are extremely easy to understand; the hard part is applying them to your situation. It is not hard to understand, but you may have to change some things in your life to see the results. I am excited for you for taking this step in your journey, and getting this necessary information to keep you going, growing, and thriving. Nothing can stop the man or woman with a made up mind to win. If this is you, well you have surely picked up the right book. Let's get started!

LAW #1

The Belief EFFECT

"We are not here to make believe, we are here to believe we can make it!" -Guru Singh

Chapter 1

LAW #1

"The BELIEF Effect"

"If I have the belief that I can do it, I shall surely acquire the capacity to do it even if I may not have it at the beginning. - Gandhi

    If it is not in you, then it can't come out of you. You can't produce what you have not first created a strong conviction for on the inside. I think one of the biggest mistakes people make in getting started with a new venture or learning a new skill is that they may have a conviction, but they do not wait until the conviction is strong before attempting to get others to believe in them. If you want to become a Champion in any field or endeavor, you have to first believe with unwavering confidence that you have what it takes.

    I would like to start by telling you how I personally utilized several techniques for strengthening my belief in what I am going after. I had to overcome many odds to get even a slight upper hand on my competition. As a young teen growing up in an extremely toxic environment in Milwaukee, Wisconsin, I held on to a strong belief in myself and my abilities, despite my circumstances. In the midst of growing up and trying to finish school, it seemed as if every obstacle that could possibly exist was against me. The neighborhoods were filled with despair, crime, and drugs, while my parents were doing their best to make ends meet. Now, you may not be able to relate to this, but I am sure you have your own obstacles and problems to fight through, so stay with me for a moment. When all you see is drugs, alcohol, and violence everywhere, and as we say it back home, you feel "broke, busted, and disgusted," it is very easy to lose hope and belief that you can make it out.

I state this fact only to show that I grew up just like the masses of young Black men in America; poor, and in a crime and drug infested environment with little to no opportunities; being severely stereotyped and witnessing substance abuse daily. Sounds like an unconquerable situation, right? Well, not to the person with an imagination! While most of my peers were cutting school and not caring much about their grades, I figured in the back of my mind that school was probably going to be my ticket out. I believed within myself that if I work hard enough, I would be able to not only better my circumstances, but also better the circumstances of those connected to me. There is something powerful about someone who can use their imagination to substitute for their current reality, until what they are imagining becomes their reality.

I wrote this book to encourage those who are losing hope that their situation will ever change. I would like to see a shift take place for young people who are receiving their education at underfunded public schools, and young African Americans who grew up like me to realize that there is more in life to look forward to. We have to support them in believing there is more out there for them, and help guide them in strengthening their belief in themselves, for this could be the difference in them becoming a victim of their environment or becoming victorious in life. I could have easily been a victim of my environment, and when I say easily. I mean EASILY! It is not hard to get hooked up with the wrong crowd, and turn to the streets before turning to school. It is easy to start chasing ladies who do not mind getting involved sexually, and start popping out kids left and right; this is not hard at all. It would not have been hard at all to see the money, cars, and clothes that the drug dealers in the neighborhood flaunted and chase that lifestyle. I lived it, and I know how easy it is to get caught up, so for those of you who have probably experienced something similar, I know about the challenges you face.

I personally wanted more, so I began to search for better circumstances. I took my grades very seriously while in school, and from the 9th to the 12th grade, everybody knew me as "4.0 Will," because I was the only Black kid getting 4.0 grade point averages, but seemingly never took a book home or did any homework. I was having fun like everybody else; I just took care of school first. I also loved music from listening to my dad rap, so every day, I would attract crowds by freestyling at the lunch table at my high school in Milwaukee. While in 9th grade, my homeroom teacher, Mr. Bull, had heard about my talents and encouraged me to enter some freestyle competitions. The cost to enter was $25, and not only did I not have the money, but I did not think I was good enough yet. I will never forget that he said, *"Will, I'll go ahead and pay for you to get in it, just go for it!"*

    Before continuing the story I must say this taught me at a young age that sometimes other people may see more in you than you see in yourself. At times we need others to help us strengthen our belief in ourselves. I also have to add that what made it the more special was he is a white man who never seen color but showed me love, almost like I was his own son. I am eternally grateful for what he deposited in me, teaching me more than just math but real life lessons. This is a man who really cared about the children that he taught and he continues to extend the same love for we are still friends to this day. Continuing the story; I entered the competition and, sad to say, I lost in the first round. However losing ignited me like never before. It helped me to develop this confidence to do whatever it would take to never lose again!

    After losing the first one, I went on to enter more and more rap competition events as well as many random street battles, and I started winning them all. By the time I had turned 18, I had developed a reputation as the "Freestyle King of Wisconsin" all over the city. Music was my first love, and I wanted to be the best I could be. I remember getting close to graduating from high school, and that same home room teacher, who had by then been promoted to an administrator, encouraged me to go to college. Him and another administrator, Mr. Weaver, sat me down and said, *"You should get out of here and go to college."* At the time, my grades were pretty phenomenal despite my circumstances, so I could get accepted to almost any university in the country, and I was receiving a lot of support for my music. I truly believed that I could go be successful if I left our small city, so I began to look into some out-of-state universities. This is just a brief story of how my journey began, and I hope it encourages you to stick to what you believe in.

I began to ponder what would be the best place for me to excel academically, as well as be successful in music. The year was 2005, and the city of Atlanta was beginning to grow very rapidly with opportunities for African-Americans, particularly in the entertainment field. I decided I would apply to one of the schools in Atlanta, and hope and pray that I got in. At the time, all I had was a belief inside me that said, *I will win; I just have to get out of Milwaukee first.*

Applied Belief

I decided I would take the opportunity to make a change for better, and I applied to Clark Atlanta University. I must add that I did not know anyone who lived in Atlanta; I had no contacts or family in the area. However, I was determined to get out of my current environment and leave the nest of a chaotic household to embark on my own journey. Once I got a letter from Clark that explained that I was accepted into the school and the dorms on the campus, I was ready to take the show on the road. I was 19 years old when I packed up all my clothes in my 1996 Grand Prix and jump on the road, headed towards Atlanta. I was not sure if my car would be capable of getting me through the 13-hour drive and over 800 miles, but I just believed it would. I drove all the way down there by myself, with only $600 in my pocket and no idea of how I would pay for school or housing. Talk about belief!

Belief is no good if you just allow it to stay dormant inside you. You have to go out and exercise your belief before you see results. As a 19-year-old kid going into the unknown, I was very terrified and unsure of the outcome; however, I thought to myself, *"if I fail, I can always go back home, so what do I have to lose by trying?"* When you come to a place of nothing to lose, and everything to gain, you will begin to step outside yourself like never before! I encourage high school and college students in their freshman and sophomore years to go to an out-of-state school away from home, to get away from the familiar and dive into the pool of unlimited opportunities.

The Struggle with Belief

I did finally make it to Atlanta after completing the brutal road trip alone. After being greeted by the staff and placing my clothes into my new dorm room, I was hit by a very harsh reality; I quickly realized I could not afford to be there. Do not tell anyone I told you this, but first off, I did not know Clark Atlanta University was a historically black private college (which means the tuition was high and government loans were not available). I did not know much about college at all, so I did not understand the process of enrollment and applying for private loans. I was the first in my family to go to a university of this caliber, so I had no guidance in getting properly situated. To add insult to injury, I begin to see how all the other students had their parents with them helping them get settled into their dorms; their parents, who had taken the road trip with them, and would be helping them through the process of getting enrolled.

Due to needing private loans to get situated and not having any established credit to take out those loans in my own name, I needed a co-signer. Everyone I called and asked to cosign for me was denied due to bad credit reports, and I was running out of options. As the last day approached, I began to get discouraged, because I had drove all the way down to Atlanta and now would have to go back home a failure. I was crushed! I remember the night preceding the deadline; I called my dad and just begin to cry, because I had run out of options. I remember him just saying, *"Stop all that crying, you just have to do what you have to do."* I felt like he did not understand that all of my dreams had been crushed; my belief had begun to waver, and I really began to see how unfortunate I really was compared to others who were there.

The next morning, I woke up and began to pack my bags and got ready to take the heart wrenching, disappointing, dream-crushing trip back home. After praying that night, I just decided to accept whatever happened and deal with it. Surprisingly, I got a phone call as I was packing my car back up. It was my aunt, who called to tell me she was able to get approved for the loan, and I did not have to go back home. That became the greatest day of my life; I cried tears of happiness, because I realized that I would not have been there had I not held on to my belief that it was possible to change my situation. I still get emotional thinking about that encounter, because your belief will always be tested and tried. I will even take it a step further; there will be many things that will come to completely shatter your belief, but if you remain focused, your belief will be strengthened to greater heights.

A Great Idea

I am going to tell you a quick story of what I did while in college to start my first business, and how I begin to gain tremendous momentum for my company, while still working on my degree and being involved in several organizations on campus. After going to Clark Atlanta for a year, I transferred to Georgia State University, where the tuition was more affordable, and I could focus more on my career. One day after leaving the bookstore, I realized I had spent over $700 on textbooks that would be almost worthless to me within 3 months. I could not believe how expensive college textbooks were, and realized that someone needed to do something about helping people like me get our money back.

That is when I got the idea of a textbook exchange website, where people can buy, sell, and trade textbooks with each other. Opportunities for advancement are usually all around us, if only we would pay more attention to them. The greatest opportunities to get ahead are usually the most obvious things that's in our face daily, but we always talk about how someone else should do something about the problem. If you are able to recognize problems around you that need solving, and you are not afraid to work towards a solution to the problem, you will be a Champion in your finances.

Continuing with the story, I decided the website would launch at my school, and then I planned to expand to other schools later. It sounded like a great idea; the only problem was I knew nothing about websites, nothing about business, had no partners, and most importantly, had no money. All I truly had was this great idea that I knew could help a lot of people, but I was not sure how I would bring it into reality. Have you ever been there before? If so, take notes on this section about taking an idea or dream and taking it from the belief stage to reality. If you follow some of these instructions, it will work 100% of the time. These are guaranteed principles used by some of the wealthiest individuals to ever walk this planet!

During the same time of me coming up with this idea, I was reading a book called, *Think and Grow Rich*, by Napoleon Hill–a book that should be read by every person that wants to become a Champion professionally. After you finish reading my book, if you have not yet done so, you should go and get Napoleon Hill's book, because it is the most popular and most effective book ever written on personal and professional success (you can download the pdf for free; the audio book is available as well). In Chapter 2, Hill spoke in detail on the importance of desire and how it is the starting point to all achievement. I came across a passage in the book that encouraged people who were looking to make a specific amount of money to write down, on a piece of paper, how much and what they planned to give back in return for achieving that goal. Instead of a specific amount of money, I focused on my business idea, and I immediately typed the following up and printed it out.

What is the specific idea or business?

My Statement: I am going to create a website where college students all over can come to buy, sell, and trade their textbooks, making their college experience less stressful.

How much money do I need to get this business started?

My Statement: I need $10,000 to get this business up and going.

What do you intend to give back in return?

My Statement: *If I receive $10,000 to start my business, I will give my time and knowledge to others so that they are able to accomplish great things for themselves as well.*

When do you plan to possess the money?

My Statement: *I expect to have the money to start this business within one year.*

Once this was completed, Hill explained that we should read those statements out loud at least twice a day. I did that for almost 6 months straight before trying to make any significant progress in the business. The most important thing about reading those statements was reading them with pure conviction and strong emotion. I would visualize myself already possessing the money and having a functional website. I would make myself feel as if I already had the $10,000, and my website had just gone live. Doing this everyday helped me escape for a small moment from my current reality of not having any money, dealing with car trouble, needing new clothes, and being deeply in debt due to school loans. I like to say that during this process, I tricked myself into believing I really could make it happen, and allowed myself to see beyond my circumstances. At the time, I did not realize I was strengthening my belief in accomplishing this project. I did not realize I was programming my mind with specific things I wanted to accomplish. If you are not specific enough, it will be difficult for your mind to create a picture for you and begin to show you where to find resources for accomplishing your goal.

This may seem like a tedious task, but it actually did not take long to type up the statements, and it was actually the most important step in the process. Each time I read those statements, I got more excited about seeing it become real. Saying those statements helped deal with my natural insecurities and feelings of being inadequate to take on such a large project. I stopped caring that no one in my family had ever started their own business before; I stopped caring that I had come from a poor family and environment where most would be happy to find a job, let alone create a business. I stopped caring that I did not have any money saved and had no one to even help me with all the work that needed to be done. I stopped caring that I had no mentors, no resources, and no team, but I told myself I would find everything I needed.

The first step to starting any business, new venture, new organization, new album, or creating a new product is to believe that it is possible for you to accomplish it. Most people never get out of the idea stage, because they have not created enough belief within themselves to attack the challenge with the fierceness that is required. After six months of saying those statements out loud each day, there was no one in the world who could tell me that this was not about to happen. I had strengthened my passion for getting the project done to such a great extent that I could not stop talking about it everywhere I went. If you want to be a Champion, your imagination must be greater than how things look around you. If it is not, you will never make it–and I do mean never!

Do you Want it Bad Enough?

This exercise of saying these statements out load daily truly was the most powerful thing I could have done in building up my confidence to make this happen. If you are not willingly to write down these 4 little statements and say them with conviction every day, then to be brutally honest, you really do not want it bad enough. The thing I admire most about Kobe Bryant is his competitive nature. He always seems to have the greatest belief that winning is possible, more so than anybody else on the court. Whatever he did to internalize greatness and strengthen his belief in himself has surely worked against tremendous odds. What did Oprah have to do to believe in herself and her projects so much that she is now a multi-billionaire, and also an international icon in the entertainment business? These two individuals, whether on the court or in the boardroom, have unshakable faith in their abilities and ideas, and will not accept no for an answer. I consider Kobe and Oprah both to be Champions in their fields, and they are Champions because they have the ability to believe in things most people would not have the confidence to believe in. At the time of writing this, Kobe Bryant had passed his idol, Michael Jordan, on the all-time NBA scoring list. Are you serious? You can't tell me this man did not spend countless hours in the gym working on his game, imagining that one day he would pass his idol Michael Jordan. Now this dream and passionate journey has become a reality for him. There is unlimited power in belief!

The Belief Effect

I have learned over time that when a person truly believes in something and speaks with pure conviction about the subject, it can make others believe also. I remember after my six months of saying the statements out loud that I had made a goal to find a partner to help, who I would probably give 40% of the business. I had my eye on one of my classmates who was younger than I, but very involved socially on campus, and seemed like the perfect fit for a business partner. One day, I asked if we could meet to chat about a business opportunity, and he agreed. While sitting in a conference room, I began to present the idea to him, explaining in detail how we could bring it to the campus and the money we could possibly make. This was the first time I had spoken in-depth and detail about the idea, because I wanted it to remain exclusive. However, as I was speaking, I noticed how much passion I had for the idea, how easy it was for me to speak on the subject with complete conviction that it would work. I noticed that I was not stuttering, was not nervous, and my excitement was certainly rubbing off on him. Before I could even finish my presentation, I remember him saying, *"I'm in!"*

This is what I like to call the "Belief Effect." In essence, it is your strong conviction of a thing rubbing off onto others. However, if you do not put in the time to strengthen that belief, the effect will not be as powerful. I was so excited when I saw this concept at work, because I felt as if now I was making progress, and although we still did not have any money, no expertise with websites, and not even a solid name for the website, I felt that I was one step closer to seeing it on the market.

If I had not spent six months prior to that meeting speaking out loud what I wanted to achieve, I do not know that I would have been able to convince my classmate to come on board. I had harnessed a new power that day; a power I like to call the "Belief Effect." I realized that the stronger my belief was in something, the more I could convince someone else to believe in it too. If you do not truly think your idea or dream can become a reality, people will be able to sense that very easy, and will write you off as just another dreamer. If you want to be a Champion in your career, those around you need to sense that you mean business each time they are in your presence.

Barack Obama's 2008 campaign was a perfect example of this principle at work. Obama believed in himself to such a high degree that he was able to convince an entire nation that it was time for a change; as a result, he became the first black president inaugurated in the United States. Now that's some belief! He believed in his campaign so much that he was able to convince people–White, Black, Latino and others–to support him in his goal. People put up their hard earned money to support him. A countless amount of hours of people's time was sacrificed to help him succeed in his goal as well. This was the "Belief Effect" at its finest. If people are not willingly to put up their money or their time, then they truly do not believe in you or your cause. It is your job to believe it so strongly that others get excited about doing whatever it takes to help you reach it.

After me and my new partner worked on our business plan, I knew I had to do something to help strengthen his belief in the project as well. I decided the first thing we should do was put our money together and get a logo made right away. After coming up with the appropriate name for the website, we paid a graphic artist $150 to make our logo. When the logo was finished, our eyes just lit up when we saw it. It was like watching your baby walk for the first time. We were watching our idea come to life. If you have a new business or organization you are looking to start, I encourage you to get the logo done first before you do anything else. If you do this, it will take your idea out of your head and bring something tangible to look at. I would stare at my logo every day and just imagine it being plastered all over the campus. Both my partner and I had set the logo as the screen saver on our smart phones, as well as the background picture on our laptops. We would see that logo everyday all day, and that strengthened our belief that it was a real business getting ready to hit the market.

Next, we began to set up meetings with friends and families to ask if they would invest; I was anxious to put the "Belief Effect" to the test again. We gave presentations for our families and were able to raise money. We also entered a business pitch competition at the school and won the first place prize of $250, because we had mastered our pitch. Our belief and passion for this business had become so strong that you could put us in front of anyone, and we would be able to wow them with the potential in the idea. The "Belief Effect" was working like a charm.

Always be Ready

After we had brought together our personal finances as an investment, along with the money we raised from friends and families, we had about $3000. It was not quite the $10,000 I had been looking for, but it was certainly enough for us to get started with website production. We found a developer to create a website for us within our budget, and within six to eight months, we finally had the website we had been working so very hard to get. The problem was it would take more money to market the website to the public, and to make matters worse, we were not completely satisfied with the product. The way we envisioned it in our minds was not how it was delivered to us by the programmer. It was obvious that we needed a larger budget to acquire a more experienced developer who could create the high quality website that we were expecting. I had finally brought my idea into reality after two years of long nights and stressful meetings, just to realize I still had much further to go in making the idea a successful one. Yes, if you want to become a Champion, you have to learn to appreciate your small successes and never let go of what you believe in.

One day, I was referred by a friend to get my income taxes done by a local tax preparer, who also happened to be a great business man and savvy investor. I set up a meeting to go see him, so that he could prepare my taxes. When I entered his office and we began to talk, his demeanor seemed to be very laid back. He was a young guy, seemingly a couple years older than I; however, it was very obvious that he was doing very well business-wise by the look of his office and established name. I noticed he was supervising about five other employees simultaneously, while conducting our meeting. Growing up in Milwaukee, where all the young, black, successful men I encountered had all been drug dealers or involved in some illegal sort of business, this amazed me and inspired me to a great degree.

As we began to talk about my tax situation, I explained to him that I had started a business recently, and I was not sure if I could get any tax breaks. He asked, *"What kind of business is it?"* I explained the nature of the business briefly and very unenthusiastically, and then attempted to ask another question about my tax situation. Before I could finish my question, he asked, *"Do you have a website?"* At that point, I am thinking to myself, *why is he asking me about my website?* Also, I was thinking about how I really did not like the website we had, and was not sure how I felt about showing it to him, but what harm would it do? He pulled it up right away and began to look over it and ask more questions. I began to wonder why we were no longer talking about my taxes, and had completely shifted our conversation to my business venture. Next, he said something that sparked my enthusiasm and brought me into complete focus on the opportunity. He briefly explained, *"I am looking over your site because I am also an investor, and the type that will write you a check tomorrow if I see something I like."* Feeling the pressure of now needing to impress this investor sitting right in front of me, I began to think about "The Belief Effect," and how I needed to tap into it then!

I began talking to him about the potential of bringing it to my school, our marketing strategies, and also potential revenues. The six months I had invested in saying those statements everyday was paying off, because I was speaking with so much confidence and conviction that, as a result, we spent the entire meeting talking about my idea. I explained to him that we needed a new website and we needed money to market the website around campus. He asked how much we needed, hesitating briefly because I was not sure I should ask for the full amount that I felt we needed. A few seconds later, I gained my courage and said, *"We are going to need about $10,000 to get everything we need."* Surprisingly, he said, *"Okay, let's set up a meeting and see if we can make that happen for you."* Two days later, we met at the Commerce Club in downtown Atlanta and hashed out the details of the deal. We settled on 20% of the company for $10,000 cash for start-up. The day after we signed our contracts for the deal, he wrote us a check and the rest is history. This was obviously a great victory for our young company.

I am more than convinced that I was able to secure this deal because of the time I invested in becoming emotionally attached to the success of this company. It took a few days for me to actually accept that a young boy that grew up around nothing but drug dealers, alcoholics, and drug abusers had just made a deal of that caliber. I had started with an idea, and now I was a business owner with two partners who believed in me, while also finally having the money I needed for getting things off to a great start. $10,000 may or may not be a lot of money to you, but the amount of money received is not why I tell you this story. I tell this story because I was able to go through the process of bringing something out of idea form into reality. I said out loud for six months that I needed $10,000, not knowing where it would come from, and all of a sudden 2 years later I have someone writing me a check! After about another six to eight months, an upgraded and updated version of our site went live, and we had our first group of users sign up to use our service.

I continued to face challenges with making the venture successful, dealing with the ups and downs of business; however, I tell this story to help you see the effect your beliefs can have on others. I encourage you to write down your simple statement as well and make sure you are very specific about what you want. Every day first thing in the morning say it out loud and also before you retire at night. The "Belief Effect" opened me up to a whole new world of opportunities; a world where all things are possible for those who will not take no for an answer, and where there is more than enough money out there for any person who has the ability to communicate their ideas effectively. The one thing every great Champion has in common is they all believe that they are going to be great, because being great does not happen by accident; it's something you have to have inside of you first!

LAW #2

The Real YOU

"Why are you trying so hard to fit in, when you were meant to stand out?" -Unknown

Chapter 2

LAW #2

The Real You

*"Don't wait until the end of your life to find out who you really are." –
Unknown*

*"Don't change so people can like you. Be yourself and the right people
will love the real you."* Unknown

What is it that a Champion possesses that allows them to excel above the masses? How are they able to captivate the attention of people seemingly effortlessly? Why do they look happy and fulfilled although the work they engage in may be burdensome? Well, these questions have truly peaked my curiosity and caused me to look deeper into the lives of those who have achieved success in all areas of life, to find what it is that makes them shine so bright. You are reading this book, so that probably means you must be curious as well. How can you go from where you are now and excel to immeasurable heights of success? Why have things not been working out for you the way you have planned? If you can answer the following question and act on it right away; you will begin to see immediate results in your career and life. The question is, *"What is it that you have discovered about yourself that you have not found anywhere else in the world?"*

This may seem like an obvious question, but I talk to people every day who live their lives in a routine fashion, never finding anything to uniquely identify with. What is it that can keep you up all night trying to figure out? What would you practice for hours upon hours until it was mastered regardless of whether or not you were paid for it? What is the issue that sets you on fire each time you encounter it and has you wondering why no one is doing anything about it? There is a saying that, *"If your job is to do the thing you love the most, you will never work a day of your life."* I believe in this saying. I believe to truly be considered a Champion, financial or tangible success alone does not make you a Champion. For example, if a man or woman is in a career that he/she does not enjoy but makes a huge salary, then in my eyes, this person is just as much of a loser as someone who never decides to get up and do anything with their lives. If you are not excited about your work or do not feel a deep connection to what you are doing, then my advice is to stop doing it at your first opportunity.

I am not encouraging any of you to quit your jobs, but what I am suggesting is that you find what you love doing first before you decide to invest your entire life into someone else's dream. Greatness is in you as you read this book, but the question is: what is it that you will be great at doing? There is a price to be paid for greatness, and you have to ask yourself, *"In what field or area would I be willing to put my all into and pay the price to be great?"* Most people who become exceedingly great in a skill, trade, or particular area of expertise develop an unprecedented love for what they do, and feel as if they have been born specifically to perform that task. They feel a deep sense of purpose while performing, and never cease wanting to get better at their craft.

Deep Purpose to Keep Focus

What does the word purpose mean? Webster explains the definition as the reason for which something is done or created, or for which something exists. After talking to thousands of people about reaching their potential, I have learned that the majority of people have a deep sense within to fulfill some purpose in their lives. Have you ever felt that way? That there is something more you should be doing? There is something more you should be getting prepared for? You have a unique purpose to accomplish as you breathe air, eat food, and live daily. You have been given gifts and talents that you should be developing every day that I hope you have not decided to let lie dormant. Champions do not let their unique gifts and talents lie dormant. True Champions are up before everyone else, working on their gifts and always willing to go the extra mile if necessary.

If you do not believe you could give your all to a specific area and focus on becoming as skilled as you possibly can, then I have some bad news for you: you will never be a Champion at anything. Once you have the belief that you can be great, you next have to find what you naturally gravitate towards, and what naturally holds your interest. Is it sports? Is it business that excites you? Are you interested in medicine or photography? It could be something less obvious, like knitting clothes, or taking care of endangered species. You might love to play chess for hours straight, or how about having an ear for hearing great music? You will know you have found your niche when:

Your passion in this particular area will be obviously much stronger than that of your peers or others in the field. You just seem to be the most enthusiastic about getting to work, no matter what time of day or circumstance. When you speak on the subject, it is with great authority and care for the subject. You might hear people around you say, *"It does not take all that."* At times, you will become frustrated with the fact that even though things may be extremely challenging, you are not able to let things go. Your love for this area is obvious to those around you, and appears to be obsessive in nature.

You are at your creative peak when working on this particular task. Your mind seems to be performing at its highest levels when you are doing this particular task. Mistakes are easily recognized, and your problem solving skills become greater in this area. You are able to see opportunities that most others are not paying attention to. Instead of just using your eyes, you are able to see what others are not paying attention to with your mind's eye.

When we as human beings begin to operate at a heightened level of creativity while working on something we care about, true happiness is not far from this place. These creative ideas are like sparks that send an electric shock to the body that get us more and more excited each time we come up with another great idea.

Time seems to speed up once you begin working in your niche.
I'm sure you've heard the saying, *"Time flies when you are having fun."* So it also is with your niche, because I have noticed that when you are engaged in your purpose, it is very hard to stare at the clock. There are usually never enough hours in the day. Your husband, wife, parents, or friends usually have to pull you away from your work so you can take a break. It may be hard to understand at the moment, but if any of these things has happened to you before, it is a sign that you are becoming a Champion in that area.

You will not accept anything half done or not perfected.
Champions, I have noticed, are what most people would call perfectionists. Anything short of perfection becomes completely unacceptable. You will be up all night trying to get it right. The things others may not see will still agitate you greatly, and cause you dissatisfaction until the problem is fixed. This is the attribute I least enjoy about myself, because being a perfectionist is time consuming. While most in your field will settle and be happy with exceptionally good, Champions are always striving for exceptionally great!

When Reality Hits Hard

If you are over 18, then you have probably experienced some level of hardship at some point of your life. We all know life is not easy, and we all have to struggle and fight to survive. Have you ever lost a loved one and felt as if you no longer wanted to live yourself anymore? Have you ever been laid off from a job and then had no idea how you were going to get your bills paid? For my younger readers, have you ever been put out of your home because of disobedience and felt all alone and unloved? Well, these types of bad situations happen all the time, and will continue to happen the older you get. Life can sometimes beat an individual up so badly that they stop dreaming completely. They let go of what they had a passion for, and just decide to accept their lot in life of working paycheck to paycheck to stay afloat. I see this most often in young men and woman who end up having children at an early age, forcing them to grow up much faster than they probably should have. The great responsibility of being a parent has forced them to put their dreams on hold, and focus on raising their child.

When you have mouths to feed, you cannot just stay at home all day and write poems if that is your passion, especially if you are not getting any compensation for it. It is hard to focus on recording your next album when first, you are not sure if it is going to sell at all, and second, the money spent on your album could be used to buy pampers and baby food. The older you get, the more responsibilities you begin to take on, and the harder it becomes to go after your dreams and passions. I estimate that 85-90% or more of this nation's population is working a job or in a career that they have no interest in whatsoever, but are doing so to make money. If you want to become a Champion, you will first have to find that particular thing that you love to do, whether you got paid or not, and become great at that thing. Self-made millionaire Farrah Gray says, *"Build your own dreams, or someone else will hire you to build theirs."* Mark Twain said, *"The two most important days in your life are the day you are born and the day you find out why you were born."*

The awesome thing about becoming great at what you love to do is you get to name your own price. How would you feel if you were able to dictate how much you got paid for your services? Your boss no longer tells you how much they are willingly to pay, but you are now letting your boss know how much you are willingly to accept. This is only effective if you are truly doing something unique that cannot be seen or received by anyone but you. That is the benefit of finding your purpose and becoming an expert in that field. The problem is that life has gotten in the way for most of us, and instead of seeing a bright future of happiness and fulfillment, we turn our attention to worrying more about just surviving day to day. So I say to the young mom who may have a passion to be a chef or a great recording artist: keep fighting for your dream! You may have to take that job during the day and take care of the baby in the evening, but the second that baby falls asleep, start practicing your craft.

Don't Accept IT!

Losing a close loved one can be very difficult and detrimental in anyone's life. This can cause people to lose hope in their talents, lose the drive to finish what they started because their loved one will not be able to see it, and cause a person to just accept what life deals out. Life will sometimes deal an ugly hand, but you have to learn to continue to play to win. I personally feel I was dealt an ugly hand at the start of my life; I just made the decision that, by any means necessary, I would not accept it. Not knowing where your next meal is coming from without a doubt stifles creativity and short circuits your passion. Working the same job week in week out with no excitement, or going through the same weekly routine all year, can also short circuit your passion and cause you to stop dreaming. However, if you truly want to be a Champion, you have to stay excited about the future.

A Champion looks at their current circumstances and sees it as preparation for where they are going. Although it may be a hard life with hard work and hard decisions; a Champion can feel in their heart that they are getting prepared for something enormous. The biggest difference I see between Champions and losers is that Champions are always preparing for something that they may not see going on currently in their lives. Losers accept life as it has been handed to them and decide they have nothing greater to prepare for. This is a great tragedy that I witness daily, especially in old friends who are still doing the same things we did back when we were in high school. They have accepted whatever the world said they should be, and for my young Black friends, the world says they should be criminals, who are uneducated drug users–but I believe they can be much more!

The Rest of Your Life

Muhammad Ali said something I will never forget; he said, *"I hated every minute of training, but I said, don't quit! Suffer now and live the rest of your life as a Champion."* I do not know if there are many people walking this Earth who don't know the name Muhammad Ali, or have not heard stories about the greatness he displayed throughout his life. Ali understood that I AM Champion because I chose to prepare to be one! While in the gym, he probably did not know he would face fellow Champions George Foreman or Frazier in the future, but he prepared himself as if he did not care who he faced. Ali's tenacity was unlike anyone before him at the time. It was not so much Ali's boxing ability that made him the greatest, in my opinion; it was his attitude, confidence, and tenacity that were unmatched during his reign at the top. Ali always remained confident in his abilities, and did not hide his uniqueness. He was very outspoken on issues he believed in, and did not care what others had to say about it.

Tunnel Vision

When you are unique, then you will stand out from the normal way things are done. Standing out from the crowd leaves you vulnerable to the criticisms of others. While I am all for constructive criticism, you have to be careful of whose advice you take. When you are unique, you are probably doing something no one has ever seen before, so listening to your instincts more than people becomes extremely vital. Unless your instincts and what people are saying are lining up (they won't in most cases), then you should not care what they say about what you are doing. If you want to become a Champion in a chosen field or specific area in your life, then you will need to develop what I would like to call, "Tunnel Vision."

Have you ever been driving through a tunnel on the highway and noticed once you went inside you were completely isolated from the rest of the world? You look to your left, you look to your right, and you cannot see anything but the walls, so this forces you to keep your eyes on getting to the other end of the tunnel. The idea is to stay focused enough to keep you looking straight, until you make it to the end of the tunnel. Most people allow too many distractions in their lives, which impairs their ability to develop this "Tunnel Vision." Sometimes, we as humans have the tendency to try to be great at everything, and this is just unrealistic. If you want to become a Champion, you have to develop "Tunnel Vision" to a ridiculous degree in one task, and one task only. While still taking care of your important responsibilities of life, you have to become insanely determined to see your vision come to pass.

Most of us also care too much about what people think. If you truly want to be a Champion, you cannot get bent out of shape each time someone has something negative to say about you. Newsflash: the top can be very lonely at times, and not everybody is going to be happy to see you there. You will have to be able to sense if what people are saying to you stems from love, or if they are trying to pull you down. However, I would like to reiterate the importance of constructive criticism that may help you see what you are not doing well, but this should come from people who you know genuinely have your best interest in mind. You will probably only have a small number of these people in your life. Most people who will be criticizing you most likely see the greatness in you as well and become jealous, envious, or just completely do not understand where you are coming from; as a result, it will be hard for them to relate to you.

It's not for Everybody

Continuing the conversation on being bold with your uniqueness and not allowing what others think of you to discourage you, it is important to understand that not everyone is going to like you. If you are like me, then you probably try to get along with everyone, and take pride in being a likable person. This is fine in your everyday social life, but when it comes to getting down to Champion business, we have to understand that not everyone is going to like what we are doing. What we are offering is not for 100% of the population. A mentor of mine gave me a powerful lesson in this when he said, *"50% will not like what you do, 25% will love what you do, and the other 25% can be swayed either way according to your actions."* It does not matter what your product or business is, not everybody is going to love what you are doing. Coca Cola is one of the greatest companies of all time, and although it may seem as so, not everybody in the world drinks Coke. Wal-Mart is, without question, the greatest retail chain currently operating on this Earth, making billions of dollars annually; even with their colossal success some, still prefer Target over Wal-Mart. Wal-Mart put a lot of people out of business, but they did not put everybody out of business. This is important to understand, because although you may begin to develop a significant following, realize that you will not convert everybody over to your ideals.

If you are striving to become a Champion in business, you will need to identify your target market, and focus on them first. Remember, 50% of those that come in contact with you will not like what you do period, 25% will love what you do, and the other 25% can be swayed either way. I made up in my mind, with all of my energy, to go after the 25% who can be swayed, and continue to satisfy the 25% who already see value in what I offer. These percentages are obviously simplistic, but they are also very modest. The 50/25/25 rule is a worst case scenario for all who are starting from scratch with a new project they wish to deliver to the public. Obviously, if you already have in mind that half the people will not like you anyway, you will not get so discouraged when you come across people who do not care about what you are doing. You will certainly come across people who do not see the value in what you are putting your time and energy into, but you can't let these individuals overly discourage you. Ask questions about why they are not able to see the value in what you are bringing, so that you will know what to do better next time. As Champions, we have to develop the ability to take what someone is saying about us that is negative, and transform it into a positive force to propel us to new heights.

Jesus provides the perfect example concerning this 50/25/25 rule. Although, you may or may not be a believer, the story of Jesus can still be a valuable lesson to learn from. It always amazes me how Jesus, the Ultimate Champion, could bring the same message to everyone he encountered, but some chose not to accept what he was saying for one reason or another. He went about performing miracles and miraculous healings in the presence of great crowds, but some still found negative things to say about him. The Pharisees, in particular, were intimidated by Jesus' authority and abilities, and felt that their positions as leaders in the community were being threatened. If you want to become a Champion you will need to become accustomed to people feeling intimidated by you. Greatness intimidates people, and causes them to act in very negative ways towards you to protect their respective positions. This becomes vitally important to understand, because although Jesus realized that he would not convince everyone, it did not stop him from delivering his message, even at the risk of being killed. You will face great adversity on your road to becoming a Champion; it is never as easy as it looks. The Champion always becomes a target in any field or arena, so knowing this going in allows you to be better prepared when the day comes that you are the new target on the block.

Keeping the Fire Burning

I would like to tell a brief story of a man who learned a hard lesson in letting his fire burn out. This young man, in his mid-thirties, decided to challenge himself to climbing a vast mountain. The first two days of climbing went very well for him as he progressed rapidly up the mountain. His energy levels were high, and he was performing much better than he could have ever expected. When he got tired, he would stop, eat, set up his tent, and start a fire from wood nearby. However, the higher he got on the mountain, the harder it became to find wood for his fire. He had climbed ¾ of the mountain and began to get very low on energy. He was running out of food, and at this level of the mountain, finding wood for fire was nearly impossible. He knew if he continued to climb that the possibility of finding wood was scarce, and he could potentially freeze to death once he reached the top. His fierce determination to make it to the top would not let him stop at ¾ of the mountain, so he kept climbing. After only having about an hour left of climbing to get to the top, he began to fall very low on energy. His feet and hands had become extremely cold, and he needed to find a way to warm them up as quickly as possible. He attempted to start a fire, but was unsuccessful because there was no wood in site. Unfortunately, he ended up passing out due to hypothermia and had to later be rescued by helicopter before he could reach the top.

This is a powerful story when you take a very close look at what happened here. If you want to become a Champion, you will need to learn from this story and figure out how to apply it to your life. The process of becoming a Champion is much like climbing an incredible mountain. If you have ever seen the photo of Michael Jordan winning his first NBA title, you will see him holding on tightly to the trophy with tears pouring down his eyes. He had reached the top of his mountain, and was crying tears of joy from all the hard work and dedication he had to put into getting there. However, the question we should be asking is how did he make it to the top of such a challenging mountain? The answer is, he kept his fire burning! Once you find your area of expertise, it is important to stay excited about continuing to improve yourself. The only reason Michael Jordan was able to go into the gym every morning and shoot over 300 shots was because he had a fire inside driving him towards greatness.

How do you keep your internal fire lit in the midst of adversity? First, you have to find someone else who inspires you to be the best you can be. You have to find that individual who is currently doing the things you wish to do; however, you have to take it a step further. You have to not only want to be where this individual is, but you have to strive to surpass them. A competitive drive can keep your fire burning for years and years. Second, you have to know when to step away and rest for a while. Sometimes we can work ourselves so hard that we become burned out before we can reach our goal. If you want to become a Champion, you have to know when to step away and when to come back to it. Thirdly, you just have to be creative! You have to find what is it that is specific to only you that will keep you excited about becoming the best you can be, and continually remind yourself of it.

As you climb your mountain, just like the guy in the story, most likely you will get off to a tremendous start. Your energy will be high and you will be progressing like you never would have believed. The biggest challenge is not in the beginning; it comes once you almost get to the top. It is when you are exhausted and have expended most of your energy that you met your greatest challenge to becoming a Champion. Your creativity dwindles due to lack of energy, and you begin to lose hope. It is at this point in your climb that you begin to discover abilities you did not know existed. You have to dig deeper to find wood for the fire. The same things that got you excited at the start of the climb may not be as effective at this stage. You have to dig deep within yourself and find a reason to stay excited about getting to the top. It is certainly true; the higher you get, the harder it is to find wood to keep your fire burning. If you do not keep the fire burning, you most certainly will never make it to the top of your mountain–guaranteed!

You have to keep your fire burning even in the midst of being laid off from your job. You have to keep your fire burning even in the midst of having an unexpected child. You have to be creative and keep your fire burning even in the midst of losing a close relative or loved one. It is not enough just to discover your unique purpose; that is only the first step. After you discover your purpose, you have to keep the fire burning to become the best you can be. A common denominator in all Champions is the relentless fire inside them to be the greatest, or to accomplish the task at all cost. There is no cookie cutter approach to keeping your fire burning. For me, I have always relied on prayer when all else fails to keep me energized. It may not be prayer for you, but you will need to find something to keep you keeping on as you face tremendous adversity. Do not be like the mountain climber and get almost to the top just to let your fire go out. Once you have made it that far, quitting is no longer an option; you will have to dig deep into your reserves to find a reason to keep going.

A Final Thought

As a quick review, I would like to emphasize the importance of performing self-evaluations, finding what is it that keeps you up at night and easily sparks your interest. No great achievement can be made without this important step. Also, do not let others tell you things like, *"that's not a real job,"* or *"that would never work,"* or *"you should stick to what you know."* Do not sit around and accept what life is handing out. There is no such thing as a "real job" to me; if there is not a demand currently for what you're doing, then create a demand for it. Being a Champion is challenging, and if you are not feeling challenged in any way, you are certainly not on your way to becoming a Champion. Convenience and comfort can be your greatest enemies. Think about the quote from Ali, *"I hated every minute of training, but I said, don't quit! Suffer now and live the rest of your life as a Champion."* I am sure this is the same thing Michael Jordan said to himself as he woke up every morning and headed to the gym to shoot those 300 shots. Those few years he invested into being great now allow him to live the rest of his life as a Champion. How rewarding does that sound? Lastly, never let your fire stop burning, no matter what life throws at you. You have to stay the course and keep finding new reasons to get better. It is always going to be the "Why" that pushes you more than the "What." Keep finding new "Whys," and you will be a Champion in no time!

LAW #3

Taking CONTROL

"You don't become what you hope to be in life, you become who you are in life; and you are what you think!" Unknown

Chapter 3

LAW #3

Taking Control: A Mind Thing

"Stop letting people who do so little for you control so much of your mind, feelings and emotions. – Will Smith

Thus far, we have gone into detail about the importance of belief, as well as the importance of finding your unique purpose in the world. Next, I would like to talk about a very important principle that will allow you to be effective consistently. If there is one characteristic that stands out most about a Champion, it is probably their ability to remain extremely consistent. In between your two ears is what is called the mind, and if you don't have the ability to keep it under control, you will undoubtingly have problems with consistency. Simply put, if you want to be a Champion, you will have to start thinking like one. Now, it sounds simple and yes, the concept is quite simple, but it is far from easy. This will be the hardest challenge you will face on your road to becoming and staying a Champion. It will take all of your energy and determination to get control of your mind, and to filter out all the negative thoughts. Your thinking can single-handedly take you high into the stratosphere of success, or pull you so low that you lose all hope in yourself and your abilities.

I have a brief story to tell about how I discovered this power. It was the year when I first arrived in Atlanta and began college at Clark Atlanta University. As I mentioned in the first chapter; I had come from an environment where I was exposed to drugs, violence, and despair, and was now in a city where I had the opportunity to be exposed to millionaires and their way of life. In my first business class of my freshman year, I had a teacher that would go on to change my life forever. Dr. Dennis Kimbro is his name, and you may know him, for he is a best-selling author of books that focus on strategies that some of the most successful people on Earth have utilized. Every week, he gave us a subject to write on, and he would give an award to whichever two people wrote the best paper in the class. The entire semester was almost finished, and there was only one week left, and I had yet to win the award. I submitted my paper each week, just like everyone else, and would come to class and watch as others got up to receive their award for having the best paper.

During the last week of class, I submitted my paper but decided I would not go to class that day. My roommate, Marvin, and I both decided we would not go, because we never won anything anyway, and it was the last day of class, so what would it hurt? Surprisingly, when the class was over, people were calling our phones. I remember friends of ours calling and saying, *"Will, where were you and Marvin today? Did you know that both of you wrote the best paper in the class this week?"* I was obviously shocked and disappointed that I did not go to class that day. I also thought to myself, *"I still want my award! I earned it!"* Later that day, I went to Dr. Kimbro's office to talk to him about getting my award. I was very nervous due to the fact that Dr. Kimbro was strict and could be very intimidating; I just knew he would get on me about missing class, especially since had I won on that day. I truly admired the man, and as I approached his office, I felt the intimidation dwindle, and I began to get really excited about getting a little one-on-one time with him.

When I made it in, he said, *"Congratulations, young man, on writing such a great paper, but you know you should have been in class, right?"* I nodded and replied, *"I know I should have been in class, I apologize, but I would really like to read one of your books."* Up to that point, I had not been much of a book reader in my life. Although I actually liked to read, at age 19, I had not yet begun reading books for enjoyment or for self-improvement purposes. He then grabbed a small-sized paperback book that was relatively thick. The color of the cover was navy blue and the title read, "Think and Grow Rich: A Black Choice." In the first chapter on belief, if you recall, I wrote about what I read in, "Think and Grow Rich" by Napoleon Hill that helped me prepare to start my business. Dr. Dennis Kimbro had took on the challenge of writing a follow up book to Napoleon Hill's classic to cater to the African American community (this book is also a must read regardless of ethnicity). Although I had never read a full book outside of textbooks up to that point in my life, I was ecstatic to dive into this one. He signed the book with a permanent marker and wrote, *"I see greatness in you young man."* I left his office feeling like I could conquer anything, so I spent my entire summer dissecting his book.

The Greatest Power

The book contained concepts and principles that Dr. Kimbro took from his various encounters with African American men and woman who had achieved great success. The list included the likes of Spike Lee, Jesse Jackson, Michael Jordan, Dr. Selma Burke, Oprah Winfrey, and many others. While reading about those great Champions of our time, I came across some information that would instantly change my life forever, and I wish to share it with you–for those who may have not discovered this great power in your lives yet. There was a portion in the book that talked about our ability as human beings to control our thoughts. Although I am sure I may have heard of this concept before, it did not dawn on me until that very moment how powerful this piece of information was. Up to that point in my life, I had always believed that our thoughts came into our mind at random. I had believed that in my mind, thoughts came in and out without my control. My perception was that I did not decide what I was thinking, but certain stimuli would carry my mind into different thoughts, and the thoughts and ideas themselves came to me at random. Has that ever been your perception of how the mind works? If not, that's okay; just bear with me, because I was still very young at the time.

Dr. Kimbro explained in his book that we can control and dictate what shows up on the screen of our minds. If it is okay with you, can we pause and do a brief exercise to prove this statement? First, close your eyes and think about your dream car. Think about the color of it, think about how you feel while sitting in the driver seat. Feel how comfortable the seats are as you drive to your dream job. Now stop! Put only the color red in your mind–can you see it clearly? Now place an image in your mind of you standing in front of your dream car looking at it, and it has just turned bright red. Imagine that the car alarm is going off constantly, and you have to pull out your keys to turn the alarm off. Now stop! Think about a banana, its color, and its shape on the outside. Now just imagine you are looking at a whole field of bananas, and instantly the field of bananas turns into $100 dollar bills. Now stop!

How did you feel while conducting this exercise? Did it feel a little weird at first? Did you have to first clear your mind of other things? Were you able to picture all the different things I described? Did you notice how easy it was for you to start with looking at a banana and then be able to turn a field of bananas into $100 bills? This is a powerful exercise, because if you truly paused for a moment and participated, you will realize you have the power to push other things out of your mind and place whatever you want onto the screen. I also had you stop and quickly think of something else to show the power you have to change a thought in an instant, and begin to think of something else totally unrelated. If you have ever used a smartphone or computer, you will notice that there are several applications on these devices. The device does not dictate what goes on the screen; it is the user of the device that dictates what app shows up on the screen.

The same is happening in our minds. Your mind is much like a computer that can only be useful if the person using it is putting the right things on the screen. If you want to become a Champion, learning to control what is on the screen of your mind is the most important exercise you can do–period! I say exercise, because that is actually what it is. We have to exercise our ability to control our thoughts so that we can become better at it. This takes work and daily practice. You have to intentionally decide to take certain things out of your thought life. The reason so many people are depressed is because they have not properly exercised this power in their life. Depressed people continually dwell on painful thoughts that make them feel unloved, worthless, and all alone. I have been there before, and I know that being depressed can sometimes feel like an impossible situation to get out of. I have reached some low points in my life, and felt as if I would never rise above the destructive feelings and thoughts that dominated my life daily. When you do not have money to take care of your needs, this can led to depression and the rise of self-defeating thoughts. I call them SELF Defeating, because that is exactly what it is; you are being defeated by Self. Most people are not Champions because they defeat THEMSELVES way before anyone else comes along to defeat them. This is why the importance of harnessing this power can keep your life vibrate and thriving daily. You have to decide to take control now!

You will not be great at this the first time you start trying to take control of your thoughts, just like you did not know how to ride a bike the first time you got on it; so, take the same approach here. It will take time to get good at controlling the thoughts that come across the screen of your mind. The more you practice, just like riding a bike, the more it will become second nature; and after a while, you will be able to ride the bike without thinking much about it. However, you must understand that you probably will never master this skill. It will take all of your life to get great at this skill. It is very difficult to do living in such a hectic world, with everyone competing for your attention. The important thing to note is, you can become a Champion in your thought life if you work at it daily.

The Tragedy of not Harnessing the Power

Sadly, controlling your mind actually takes work and effort to be done on our part; as a result, most people would rather let others think for them. You can never achieve the purpose for which you were created by allowing others to think for you. Most of us accept the thoughts and ideas handed down by our parents and family, never questioning the validity of such ideas. Most of us would rather let someone else make our schedule for the week than to put in the time and effort to make our own. We say we want to be our own boss and make our own schedule, but to be a great entrepreneur, you have to know how to skillfully apply this power in every area of your life. You may have all the skills, talents, and physical capabilities of starting your own business, but if you have not harnessed the power of controlling your own thoughts, then I do not recommend that you go out and try to start your own company. The greatest entrepreneurs of our time are those who are able to develop their own thoughts and ideas that most of the time go against the norm, and not allow what's popular to shift them into a different direction. A president or CEO needs to be able to say the unpopular thing when needed, and stand on this belief in the midst of turmoil and adversity. This is more difficult than finding good employees, networking with the right people, or even raising start up cash, in my opinion. The most difficult task you will undertake on your road to becoming a Champion is the task of controlling your thoughts, and standing on your unique beliefs.

There is an enormous price to pay for not controlling your thoughts, because he who has control over your thoughts has control over your life. You become a slave to whoever has control over your thoughts; so, you see why it is important that we stay in control? We relinquish our freedom when we allow the outside world to control our thoughts. I have a friend, whom I have had several conversations with about this, and I have sat back and watched her grow over the years in this area. She is a really kind-hearted person and certainly has the personality type of a people pleaser. If the normal person with a people pleasing personality is on average a four to five, then she would be on level ten, because she really takes pride in helping people and maintaining strong, healthy relationships. There were times when she would go home crying, because she was dealing with people at work who were saying negative things about her. I would then have to explain to her, *"You have a choice and must decide if you are going to let what others are saying get inside of you. You have to give people permission to hurt you, and they cannot do it without your permission, so if you feel so strongly about the situation, stop giving others so much power over your mind."*

I now hear her say things like, *"I am not going to let that situation control me; I have to move on or else it will hinder my happiness."* I smile when I see her say things like this, because I can see the maturity in her in dealing with everyday life situations. I am a strong believer in the 90/10 rule that states life is 10% what happens to you and 90% how you "choose" to respond. The key word in that sentence is "choose," which means we have to choose to be happy in the midst of tragedy and problems. Life is going to happen, and not everything that happens will be pleasant. The key is choosing our responses to what has happened, which means not letting the situation take control of us, but taking control of the situation. If you want to become a Champion, you will have to live by the 90/10 rule everyday of your life. Harnessing the 90/10 rule single handedly can qualify you as a Champion, because to be a Champion in life, you first have to be a Champion in your thoughts.

After completing the book that Dr. Kimbro gave me, it felt like I had won the lottery. The reason was because my circumstances no longer had control over me, and I now had the power I needed to overcome every negative situation I would face. Wow, I can't say enough about how vital this concept was to changing my outlook on life. I began calling all of my friends and family and telling them that I was going to be very rich one day; I know you are probably laughing at that. Although I was very broke at the time, with not an idea how I would pay for school the following year or where I would live, I still felt very rich on the inside. I started to tell some of my friends who had helped me in my time of need that I was going to make sure I took care of them in the future for helping me. I look back now and see how crazy I probably sounded, but I truly felt like I had found treasure, and became filthy rich! My wish is only to be able to pass this treasure on to you, and hopefully your life can change for the better as well.

Dealing with Real Issues

In my second year in Atlanta, I knew my aunt could not co-sign for another huge loan for me to go to school, and I had no way of paying my tuition. Most of my family was not well off and didn't have good credit, so I was stuck to figure it out on my own. To make matters worse, I had promised my dorm roommate, Marvin, that we could get an apartment together the following year. Unfortunately, I could not afford to enroll back into Clark Atlanta the following year, and we could not find an apartment, so I packed all of my things in my car again and was getting ready to head back to Milwaukee after just a year in Atlanta. I figured I would stop by my close friend Jeff's house to say goodbye before I hit the road. As I drove over his house, negative thoughts were dominating my mind. I felt like a failure and thought to myself, *"What am I going to tell everybody when I get back home? I will look like a failure."* My spirit was crushed as I pulled up to my friend's house to say my goodbyes.

Surprisingly, when I pulled into the apartment complex, I saw my former roommate, Marvin, standing over one of the balconies. He said, *"Will, I been trying to call you all day! I got approved for an apartment."* Once again, just when I had lost all hope, a miracle happened that allowed me to stay. At first this was great news, because I did not have to go home and look like a failure, but I now had new problems to face. First, I was not going to be in school that year, so the purpose of me being in Atlanta was not being fulfilled. Second, I had just agreed to be Marvin's roommate and was happy about our first apartment, but the problem was that neither one of us had a job. Marvin's mom and dad would send him money and help him the best they could, but I had no idea how I was going to pay my portion of the rent, electric, and buy food. As a result, I worked really hard filling out applications and landed three jobs very fast. It was then that things really began to get bad in my life.

One of the biggest challenges of living out of state was being so far away from my family. I'm the kind of guy that loves being around family and friends and people I am familiar with. I was still a boy when I arrived in Atlanta, so being away from family was killing me. When I first got to Atlanta, while living in the dorms, I would go home during every break and holiday to ease some of the home sickness. However, I now had three jobs and was met with a dilemma that I am sure you may be familiar with; no vacation time, no time off. This was a tough period for me mentally, because I was down about not being in school, and on top of that, I could not go home to see my family. I worked first, second, and third shift, and some days I would be so tired at work that I was almost hallucinating. To make matters worse, I was still broke with no bed, no food, no TV, and our electricity had been disconnected. As much as I tried to be optimistic at work, once I got home and sat in my room alone in the dark, eating crackers and peanut butter; it was difficult for me to keep from crying myself to sleep. I just wanted to give up and go home; I was not in school anyway, but I felt bad because if I left, I would leave Marvin hanging, and I knew he could not afford to take care of the bills by himself, so he would have to go back home too. I did not want to give up on him so I decided to stick it out.

As a result, for a year and a half, all I did was work full-time, trying to keep my spirits high as depression was attempting to rob me of my destiny. During that time, I got a young lady pregnant, and this became added pressure because I was expecting my first child, who happened to be a boy. I was excited and terrified at the same time, but I was going to handle my responsibility. When the young lady went into labor, she had a lot of complications while delivering and ended up having a stillborn delivery. I started out terrified about having a child, but it did not take long for me to become excited and begin anticipating my first child. When I found out that the baby died, I was completely traumatized for a long period of time. Yes, I was going through a lot to say the least.

I remember that after surviving over a year of grueling work just to pay bills and be broke again, I had finally been accepted into another university. The problem was that because I had not had a Georgia ID for more than a year, I was not considered a resident and had to pay out-of-state tuition. I could not afford to pay the higher cost of out-of-state tuition, which was a difference of over $6,000 per semester. I had been pretending for over a year that I was still in school. My parents, family, and friends all thought I was still in school. Sadly, no one in my family had been to visit me in three years, and I had no family in Atlanta so no one knew what the truth was. I was doing a lot of pretending when in reality, I was completely depressed and facing the greatest challenges of my life.

When I got the news that I may have to sit out of school another semester, I had lost all hope completely. At that point, I was so crushed, tired, homesick, still grieving my son, broke, and at the end of my road that I thought of taking my own life. I tell this story to help paint the picture that even I have battled greatly with negative thoughts that attempted to take me out of here. I now understand how people can reach the end of their rope where they will do something so drastic. I hear people say all the time, *"How can they do that to themselves?"* Well, I now know how it feels to just want to give up completely. I was lucky to have a friend of mine call me and encourage me to stay strong; talking me out of taking the coward way out, but everybody won't be so lucky in similar situations. That is why I encourage you now to begin to gain control as much as possible over your mind, to protect you or others from falling victim of suicidal thoughts. If you want to become a Champion in life, understand that effectively combating negative thoughts can be a matter of life and death.

A System

You should probably come up with a system for combating these thoughts. Some people meditate, some pray, and others read books such as this one. Find what works for you and what keeps your spirit lifted. Staying positive and optimistic is vital in being a great Champion in any field. It is not easy to stay positive, and it will not happen automatically. It will certainly require work on your part to stay positive in the midst of troubled times. Every morning, you will need to do something to get your mind in the right place to start your day. If you want to become a Champion, you will have to develop habits that keep your thinking elevated. It is not enough to just know about the power of controlling your thoughts. It is also not enough to just think random thoughts to keep your mind busy. Doing so will only keep you distracted from the real problem temporarily. However, we have to engage in actively thinking thoughts that inspire us, that keeps our fire burning, and that stretch us past our current circumstances.

As I said before, when I get in a situation where my thoughts are saying things like, *"You are a failure," "You might as well quit," "Nobody cares what you have to say,"* or *"Life is not worth living,"* I turn to prayer. I personally was taught by my mom that when such situations arise, we have to start praying. Most Champions believe in a higher power; not all will, and I am not saying you have to, but I personally believe that having faith in a power stronger than ourselves gives us a greater chance at success. As I sat down thinking about all that was going wrong in my life as I previously described, and how I was ready to give up on life, I had to start praying with everything in me to prevent myself from doing something to hurt myself and my loved ones. I got lots of books to keep my mind busy and in a positive focus. There is a saying that goes, *"An idle mind is the devil's workshop,"* and whether you believe that there is a devil or not, this saying is very true because when your mind is idle, you begin to think on more negative self-defeating thoughts.

An "idle" mind is a mind that is not focused or engaged in anything, but is just casually taking things day by day. Someone with an "idle" mind has not taken control of their mind, so it is said that their mind begins to be influenced by the devil. Call it what you want, if you sit around doing nothing for a long enough time, you will begin thinking about something that you probably should not be allowing to appear on your screen. For example, you may begin to think heavily about that loved one that you lost, which can cripple your psyche instantly. You may start thinking about your finances that you may not be happy with, and then begin thinking about ways to stay entertained that may involve drugs or alcohol to keep your mind busy. All these things come from not keeping your mind active and working towards the goals you have set for yourself daily.

Wrapping up

You cannot be human and not have experienced some level of attack on your mind with self-defeating thoughts. We have to be careful, because especially in this country, I believe the media is actively engaged in programming our minds to think negatively. I look at hip-hop videos, and all they show is the light-skinned big booty girl standing next to this exotic car, making the rapper appear to be a success because he has those things. Overtime, if you see those same images for years and years, you will begin to believe that is really what success and being a Champion are all about. This could not be further from the truth. It is only a way to keep us striving to achieve a false appearance of success, and not true success.

I encourage you to protect your mind from images and music that can be potentially harmful to your thought life. We can easily become attached to material things in this world because in our mind, we have been programmed from birth that these things (i.e. money, cars, clothes, jewelry) define us and are a part of our identity. If you want to become a Champion, you will need to begin to program YOURSELF and stop leaving that job up to someone else. Just like any computer or intelligent device, your brain must be programmed before it can be used. You can do the programming, or you can allow the world to do the programming, but it will be done with or without your consent. The risk you take with allowing the world to do it for you is they will not have your best interest at hand, and will probably program your mind so that you can become a useful tool to benefit them.

Have you ever thought to yourself that all of the hard work that you are putting in everyday is getting you nowhere, but is making everybody else rich? *My boss is getting richer, all the stores I shop at are getting richer, my landlord is getting richer, the daycare my child attends is getting richer, but what about me!??* Well, this next statement may sting a bit, but only to help you realize the deeper truth here. The problem is that you have not taken control of your own programming and have allowed others do it. Your mind has been programmed to work your back out helping everyone else get ahead but yourself. It may be hard to see it that way, but when you take a deep look at it, that is possibly what the root cause of your problem is. I congratulate you for picking up this book and beginning to read, because you have taken a step towards taking your mind back and, as a result, taking your life back as well. I know this is deep stuff, but if you want to become a Champion, you will need to take a deep look at why you think the way you do, and begin to make the necessary changes. You don't become what you hope to be in life; you become who you are in life, and you are what you think!

The reason I had almost reached self-destruction was from the same problem that I explained my friend was having. I had allowed my circumstances to get the best of me. Although my circumstances in that particular situation were horrific, I still should have been able to keep my composure throughout, and not be moved by the disappointments of things not going my way. Everything will not go our way, and we must accept that and learn to keep a leveled mind, whether we are up or down. Success, especially fame and fortune, can destroy your mind just as much as lack and disappointment can. The battle of the mind is fierce; money and power have the potential to corrupt your thought life, just has much as not having any power or money. The point I am making is we have to be neutral in all circumstances, allowing positive and pleasing thoughts to flow no matter the circumstances, whether they are favorable or not. If our goal is to keep up with everyone else, we are going to have a hard time being happy, because there will always be someone doing better than us. Staying in your own lane becomes critical, and being content with your own progress becomes vital.

As I wrap up this chapter, I would like to reiterate that you will never be perfect in controlling your thoughts. I battle daily with my thoughts still to this day. The difference is that since I have undergone tumultuous times, where the pressure was at its highest, problems that I encounter now don't seem so big anymore. If you want to be a Champion, you have to learn to recognize your strengths and weaknesses. I now know how to detect when negative thoughts are attempting to move in and take over my mind. The key is getting rid of them quickly before they begin to fester, because if they do fester, depression has an opportunity to show up once again; it comes from not getting rid of those thoughts before they begin to take root. As you continue on your road to becoming a Champion remember, *"You can't keep a bird from landing on your head, but you can keep them from making a nest."*

LAW #4

PAIN:

The NAME

OF

The GAME

Pain is Temporary, Quitting is FOREVER! Unknown

Chapter 4

LAW #4

PAIN: The Name of the Game

"Broken crayons still color" -Unknown

    Here's a quick story. I was at the basketball court playing some ball with friends, and we were all competing at a very high level. It was not the most pleasant experience, because in the past I have had issues with lower back pain, and I began to notice my back feeling a bit irritated. As I continued to play, I began to get a sense that something was not right with me at all. After we finished the game, I went to sit down on the bench and noticed that I could not get back up. Excruciating shots of pain began to burst throughout my lower back, and the expression on my face clearly showed that I was not feeling well. I had been dealing with lower back pain for almost five years before that incident, but that was the worst pain I had ever felt. I believe that was the *straw that broke the camel's back* as the saying goes, and not to be funny, but whatever I did on that court broke my back literally.

    I had to be helped to the car, because I could barely hold my own weight to walk on my own. Everyone kept asking, *"Are you alright?"* Normally I would respond with, *"I'm good, nothing I can't get through,"* but this was one of those times when I had to just tell them, *"No this pain is unbearable!"* At the time, I did not have health insurance, so going to the hospital was really not an option to me, because I did not want to incur the outrageous doctor bills just to be told that nothing was wrong and given pain medication. (Looking back, that is probably why the problem had gotten so bad, because I had ignored it for years without seeking medical attention.) I decided to just go home, put some ice on it, and wait for it to get better.

The Show Must Go On

Unfortunately, it was not getting better and I was bed ridden for over a week. The problem was that I had a really big event coming up that I absolutely could not miss. At the time, I had moved back to Milwaukee after graduating from Georgia State, and I had a huge event that I needed to attend back in Atlanta, where I started my bookstore business. I got an email that stated I was going to be placed on the cover of a magazine and have a two-page article written about me and my business, and I needed to be in Atlanta for the magazine's release event. You know what was going through my mind? Probably the same thing that would be going through yours if you were in a similar situation. In my mind, I'm saying, *"You can't be serious?" "Not now!" "I won't be able to make it." "How can I show up like this?" "Lord, why did this have to happen to me right now?"* I was hopelessly discouraged as I popped pain pills, used heating pads, and every home remedy I could think of with no success.

The event was three days away and I began to get worried, because my back was not getting any better. I called down to Atlanta and spoke with a friend of mine, and told her about my situation. She said that she knew a back specialist there in Atlanta that could possibly see me last minute as a favor to her if I could get there. That gave me a sense of hope, but the only problem was I had no idea how I was going to get there when I could barely walk. After getting off the phone with my friend, I laid in my bed for a couple hours, thinking about what I should do. I could not imagine missing such a pivotal moment in my life that I had worked so hard for. In my mind, I could see myself on that cover, and I wanted to be there when the magazine was released. It was the first time something like that was going to happen for me, and the first time it has ever happened to anyone in my family. Next to graduating from college, it was seemingly the most important event of my life to date.

I stopped just thinking about it; I got online and booked a plane ticket to Atlanta for the next day. While still in unbearable pain, and barely able to make it to the rest room on my own, I decided I was going to get to Atlanta by any means necessary. I could not even pack my own luggage because of my condition. I had to fight off so many negative thoughts that began to pop up in my mind, such as, *"You're 26 years old and crippled already." "You may be disabled for the rest of your life." "Everyone is going to see you looking crippled."* I realized that what I was going through what could become a midlife crisis if I allowed it to. Have you ever had negative thoughts go through your mind like that? It may not be with physical pain, but with anything that causes you to doubt yourself and who you really are? Think about that time and imagine how hard it was to get rid of those kinds of thoughts.

Continuing the story; I woke up the next morning with a mindset to face the pain and endure whatever I needed to get to that event. After being helped in the car and heading to the airport, I decided to keep my spirits high. Those taking me to the airport were worried about me traveling by myself in that condition, and tried to talk me into staying home, but they knew it was not an option. I had to suck it up and act as if I was okay, although I still could not stand for more than 60 seconds or walk more than five or six steps without collapsing. Yes, it was that bad, unfortunately. When I made it to the airport, one of the airline employees came with a wheelchair. I will never forget the way I felt as I looked around me, and everyone else who needed wheelchair assistance was at least three times my age. I began to feel very discouraged, because I truly could not make it to the loading area by myself and I had never been in that position before.

I made conversation with the person who pushed me to the loading area to hopefully make them feel a bit more comfortable with wheeling someone so young. I made sure I tipped them well to show my appreciation. I got on the plane finally, and asked God, *"Please give me the strength to make it through this."* When I made it to Atlanta, it was the same process, except Atlanta's airport was five times bigger than Milwaukee's, so being wheeled around there was much more embarrassing. I continued smiling, making jokes and being my normal self as much as I could, while enduring the worst pain I had ever felt in my life.

Get there!

I rested up, and the next day I made my way to the event. I was able to get dressed, but when I walked, it was obvious something was wrong. The pain had went from a 10 to about an eight by the time the event took place, so I had a bit of relief, but not much. I was able to stand and walk, but not too much. When I made it to the event, I tried my best to be social, but I was in a lot of pain. I smiled, took pictures, and even walked up and received my award while doing my best to hide how much pain I was in. Once the event was over, I did not stay and chat like most people did. In my mind, I knew people wanted to come and network with me afterwards because I was on the cover, but I just slipped out nice and quiet, because I needed to go rest my back.

The next day, I was taken to see the back specialist. He invited me into his home to see him, because it was a non-business day (a Sunday) and he understood it was an emergency situation. When he seen my condition and saw how stiff I was, he was very concerned. He was an Asian man who specialized in natural healing techniques. He said to me, *"Wow, this is really bad, I haven't seen someone in such dire condition in a long time."* He began to stretch my legs, because he said not stretching properly had contributed to the injury. (I know this story is a bit lengthy, but follow me–I'm going somewhere with this). He also said, *"They call me the torture doctor; I torture people for a living, but when they leave, they are usually feeling much better,"* and torture he did. He stretched my legs farther than they had ever been stretched. I just yelled while trying not to cry in front of him and my friend, because the pain was so intense. He put these suction cups on my back that were hooked to a machine, and they sucked a lot of the pressure out of my back, and released a lot of tension. When I left his home I was walking better and moving much better. After resting a couple days I was almost at 100% and able to walk through the airport on my own to get back home.

Don't Blame the PAIN

The back injury came at the worst possible time in my life. The pain that came with it was the worst I had ever felt, and it put my back against the wall. Was I going to sit at home and let it overtake me or was I going to get up out my bed and fight through it? That is the question you have to ask yourself every day. Am I going to allow the pain to stop my stride, or will I continue to fly regardless? As a man, it is very hard for me to express my feelings or show any sign of weakness. It is the nature of men to try to lead people to believe that we feel no pain, and that we are invincible, but this cannot be further from the truth. A lot of us are still carrying pain from our father's not being active in our lives, from being abused as a child, from watching our parents fight or verbally abuse each other, etc. From the way I walked, you could see I was in a lot of pain, but what about the pain you can't see? This is the pain that is festering inside that no one knows is there. I guarantee you this kind of pain has killed more dreams, stopped more plans, and destroyed more families than you can possibly imagine.

It is my belief that because a great deal of people have a hard time dealing with the pain they have experienced, they'd rather use it as an excuse not to move forward than to face it. If you want to be a Champion in life or in any area of your life, you must learn to face your pain and deal with it. Avoiding it (like I did with my back problem for five years) only makes things worse and much harder to fix later. Work on that broken relationship now while you can, and let go of the past hurt that you experienced in your life; don't let it be a disability or something that gets in the way of what you know you feel in your heart. I believe the reason there is such a small percentage of people who become extremely wealthy or extremely successful in their careers is because there are only a small percentage of people willing to go through life not avoiding pain. The majority of us want to avoid pain and stress at all costs, even if it does cost us our destiny.

The sad part about it is the pain you go through to reach your goals and destiny is temporary, but the pain of regret lasts an eternity. The pain of working for someone else all your life and not being able to give your children the things they need, hurts worse than the temporary pain that you experience in fighting for your dreams, in my opinion. I told the story about my back only to illustrate the importance of being able to endure great pain. Pain is all in the mind, and once you are able to develop the ability to allow pain to motivate you more than it discourages you, it is at that point that you will have the tools to overcome anything life throws at you!

Facing it!

Think about a Champion like Harriet Tubman. She may not be the first person that comes to mind when you think of a Champion, but her story is the perfect example of someone not avoiding pain to see a greater result. Think about how bad she would have been physically harmed if she had been caught leading slaves out of bondage. They would have stripped her of all her clothes, tied her to a tree while naked and gave her so many lashes she would probably drown in her own blood by the time they were finished. I believe she knew it was a great possibility of that happening to her, so that made her more careful. The thought of what she would experience if she got caught made her more tenacious and more determined to get the slaves back by any means necessary, and not lose one passenger.

Harriet Tubman is one of the greatest Champions of her generation, because she sacrificed herself so that others may have some kind of future. She was the Moses of her time, who did not avoid pain and the Moses for Black people of our time is Dr. Martin Luther King; a great Champion who did not have lots of money, did not drive a Bentley, and did not care to be famous, but went down in history as one of the greatest leaders ever to live. We could not begin to imagine the kind of pain that

MLK faced on a daily basis; the pain of knowing white supremacists were threatening to kill his wife and kids. He dealt with the pain of going to jail repeatedly for peaceful protest along with the pain of billy clubs, water hoses, and vicious dogs being used to hurt and discourage him and his followers from moving forward. I am sure there came a specific time when Dr. Martin Luther King Jr. was lying in his bed at night and said to himself, *"I am probably going to lose my life over this."* What's so interesting about that is when he woke up and got out of bed the next morning, he did not stop fighting for what he believed in. Where would this country be if he would have let the fear of dying, the fear of being beaten, or the fear of being humiliated overtake him and cause him to back out? Personally, as a Black man, I do not know where I would be if he did not get out of bed that next day and face the pain. When he got out of bed, he opened the door for generations and generations to come–now how powerful is that! That makes it all worth any temporary pain you endure, because the result will be everlasting.

We Can TOO!

Dr. Martin Luther King Jr and Harriet Tubman were just people like me and you. These two were alive during some of the most difficult times for Black people, so out of necessity, they stepped up for their generation. However, we are still living in some difficult times in this country. There is still a great deal of work to be done before there is peace and equality between the races and different social classes. It is okay to be successful in your career or field of interest, but the greatest Champions are those that sacrifice for others. I am not saying put your life on the line like Harriet and MLK, but what I am saying is try to fight for something that can help someone besides yourself. We live in an "all about me" society, where social media allows us to create profiles of ourselves, and we just focus on how much attention we can draw to ourselves. How much money can I make for myself? How many people can I get to like my picture? How many friends or followers can I get for my page?

We have to see past our self-centeredness and look around at how much help is needed out here. The kids in your community need help; they need role models, and they need someone to give them good advice, teach them about relationships, and be patient with them as they make mistakes. If you have children right now, notice how much your children pick up on your bad habits. They do and become what they see in you, so if you have to go through some temporary pain to change yourself so that your child(ren) can have a brighter future than you were given, do you think it may be worth it?

Something Must GO!

We talked about enduring pain; now I would like to focus on a very important principle that every Champion lives by, and that is the "Law of Trade-offs." If you want to be a Champion, you must first understand that something has to be sacrificed! In the first chapter, I spoke about how Napoleon Hill gave instructions in his book to write a statement for how much money you planned to make. If you recall, there was a question that stated, *"What are you willing to give to receive this particular goal?"* It took me a while to understand it, but now I see why it was necessary for him to place this question within the statement. It is similar to a situation in which you go to the car lot in search of a new car, and you find one you really like. You let the dealer know, and they just hand over the keys and say, *"Enjoy your new ride."* You pull off the lot with a brand new car, without paying a dime for it. This is obviously not very likely to happen, and the same concept applies to your plight of becoming a Champion.

The world we live in revolves around trade-offs and exchanges. If you want a new car, you can drive it off the lot, but you will have to give up something equal in value for it. Nothing worth having comes free, and the cost to be a Champion is just like a Bentley–it's expensive! Champions are willing to give up things that they value in their lives to pay for being great. They are willing to give up those few extra hours of sleep. They are willing to give up those weekends hanging out with friends to focus on getting better at what they do. They are willing to give up paying for that vacation to invest in their dreams instead. If you are not willing to sacrifice something of value in your life, then you cannot expect to be great at anything. You may be asking, *"How does this relate to pain?"* Well, most of the time when you sacrifice something you love or value in exchange to get prepared for greatness, it can be very painful.

Not getting enough sleep can be painful at times, and it gets extremely tough to get out of bed when you are not feeling well. Seeing all your friends seemingly having the time of their lives while you are stuck working can be extremely painful at times. Investing your money on something that is not 100% guaranteed, as opposed to spending it on something you would enjoy, can be extremely difficult and even painful. Studying when you could be on the beach, training when you could be at the movies, traveling when you could be at home spending time with the kids can all be extremely painful. However, this is how the "Law of Trade-offs" works, and no one is exempt. If you want to be a Champion, you must be willing to relinquish something that is of value to you. You will not be able to keep all of the conveniences in your life and become great.

I know you might have thought I was going to just give you a bunch of motivating quotes in this book, and tell you that if you just use positive thinking then you will have everything you have ever wanted. Well, I am a person that would actually like to see you become the great Champion that you know you can be. Telling you that positive thinking is going to get you there is only half the story. The other half is the painful part that most Champions do not discuss, and that has to do with giving up quality time with the family and fun in the sun at the beach. I am not saying that you will not have time to enjoy the fruits of your labor, but just do not forget the labor has to be put in before you can receive the fruits. We get out only what we put in, so if you do not invest the appropriate time and energy, you cannot expect to be rewarded.

Final Thought on Pain

I do not claim to have all the answers or even 1% of them; however, I can speak from my experiences. If I had not gotten out of that bed and made it to that ceremony and magazine release event, I probably would have regretted it for the rest of my life. Not to say I will not have another opportunity as such, but I would have been disappointed because it was the first. Champions do not let anything stop them from achieving their goals, and that includes pain. Pain is necessary in life, so that we can appreciate pleasure. When it comes to conquering your goals and clearing the mountains in your life, most times you will have to go through the pain before you will ever see any pleasure. There is a door with the word "Pain" on it that stands in the way of you and all your wildest dreams. Are you going to turn around and run the other way, or have you decided you will tear down the door (and any other door that gets in your way) until you achieve what's burning deep down inside?

This chapter is the part most Champions do not talk about it. You will not see the pain LeBron James endures daily as he keeps himself healthy and physically fit. He decided it is worth putting in the hours in the gym, and if you have ever worked out in the gym, well, you know it is not the most fun activity. We do not see how much pain is endured in the weight room before he steps on the court and plays like a man amongst babies. As I said before, Michael Jordan woke up every single morning and put up 300 shots. Taking that many shots, I can tell you from experience, is painful; your arms get tired and weak; and some days you just won't feel like getting up and going to the gym. However, he had a fire burning inside him that would not let him quit until he was the best. He decided the pain that he felt was worth it to be called the best in the game later, and we as Champions in training should maintain this same attitude. Do not let pain keep you out the GAME–get to work today!

LAW #5

The HEAT

"If you can't withstand the Heat then get out of the kitchen."
Unknown

Chapter 5

LAW #5

Don't Retreat from the Heat

"You never know how strong you are, until being strong is the ONLY choice you have." Unknown

In my opinion, we all have Champions inside of us, but there are two things that usually cause our inner Champion to rise into greatness, or turn into a little scared infant searching for mama's milk. The first is "pain," which I touched on in the previous chapter. If you are able to get past the temporary pain of growth, then you are now ready to take on the next element that transforms peasants into kings, and ushers those who are just considered good into extraordinarily great! Without this necessary ingredient, you can never be considered a Champion in anything. You can have all the talent in the world, but until this element has been applied, you will never be respected by your peers, followers, or friends as a Champion. Without it, you are just another person in the bunch, a statistic, a non-factor with nothing really that special to take notice of. You are probably thinking to yourself, what could this possibly be? What could be so devastating? How can I get a hold of it?

Well friend, it is not something you can get a hold of, but it has to get a hold of you. It comes with some good news and some bad news. The good news is that it is everywhere, so coming into contact with it will not be extremely difficult. The bad news is that although it is not extremely difficult to get in contact with, once you do make contact with it, your life could become extremely difficult for a time. Nothing to fear, because this same element has built great nations, saved countless lives, and has created more Champions than any other element that could possibly be thought of. So what is it that I am speaking so highly of? Well, what do you think I am talking about?

What can make you cry tears of defeat and abort your mission or goal in a heartbeat? What is it that is causing some men to run away from taking care of their children whom they have brought into this world, and at the same time has made other men strong, dependable, reliable fathers who learn to accept their responsibilities? Well, it goes by a lot of different names, but the secret ingredient that continues to develop every Champion you have seen or came in contact with can be described in one word, and that word is PRESSURE! This is one factor that does not come from inside you; instead, it is an outside force. In most instances; you cannot determine when you will have to deal with it, and on almost every occasion, it will expose you for who you really are. As a result, most of us are terrified of coming in contact with it for fear of being exposed.

Before You RUN

Now that we are on the same page as far as what this element is, let's go ahead and give it a name for the sake of this book and this conversation. I would like to call it the "Hot Seat." Now, I need some feedback from you. Think to yourself; how many times you have been put in the "Hot Seat" or been in a pressuring situation and felt completely uncomfortable and ran away fast as you can? Think about it for a second. Once you have one instance that was the most painful to run from in your mind, ask yourself what you could have done differently to stick it out. What made you run in the first place? What is it that made you shrink, not rise? What would have happened had you chosen to rise instead of shrinking? What could you have gained by rising? What did you lose by shrinking? Dig deep and ask yourself these questions about that situation that may still hurt a bit to even think about. Once you have these questions answered, you are ready to move on in this book, but I would not encourage you to continue reading if you have not thought deeply about these personal questions. Take as much time as you need, but go back in your mind to where you gave up and quit on something or someone, and relive some of those emotions, for that is part of the process of growing to be better.

Sometimes, this process pulls the Band-Aid away from a wound that has been covered, but we have to remove the Band-Aid before it can heal, or else you will continue to run for your life anytime you are in the "Hot Seat." It will become second nature, something you do without even thinking. It can become so bad that fighting back or figuring out a better way will not even be a thought, for your normal reaction to pressure will be to either cry or run, or do both at the same time. It goes without saying that this is not a characteristic of a Champion. The important issue to recognize is that everybody, and I do mean everybody, will be put in the "Hot Seat" at some point of their life, so none of us are exempt. However, what is interesting to me is how we all react differently to the heat we are being exposed to. Some of us let it burn all the life out of us until we no longer have a will to live or fight for anything, and with others it brings out a force so great and so unstoppable that everything in their way must move or get ran over! How can this be? What is it about certain people that they allow pressure to transform them into a diamond, while others let pressure and heat completely destroy their rock?

Ask yourself this question: *on a scale of 1 to 10, how good am I with dealing with pressure situations?* Go ask someone else who is close to you that has seen you in pressurized situations what they would rate you. They can probably give more of an accurate assessment, because it is difficult for us to measure our reaction while in the "Hot Seat," but spectators see everything and trust me, they are taking notice and taking notes. Your spouse, family, friends, or peers will notice anytime you are in a tense situation, and trust me, they want to know how you are going to respond. Your response could determine if someone wants to remain married to you, stay friends with you, or persists in business with you. Oh yes, being in the "Hot Seat" exposes us, and everybody around us wants to see what we are made of. I am sure you will begin to think twice before you decide to shrink next time you are in the "Hot Seat." Think about how much you can lose, think about the confidence that those around you have in you, and how that confidence can be lost based on how you respond to your pressures. From this day on, please, think hard before you run.

Get Ready to Sweat

If you cannot take the heat, then get out the kitchen; but if getting out the kitchen is not an option, then you need to prepare yourself to sweat. Let's think for a moment; when do we sweat? Some of us sweat when we are nervous. Most of us sweat when we expend a lot of physical energy and become tired. A large number of us sweat when trying to solve something that is very difficult but for the most part everybody sweats when exposed to extreme heat or expending lots of energy. These things cause us to sweat, and most of these things come from applied pressure, or what we are calling being put in the "Hot Seat." I have to be honest with you, friend; if you are not sweating at least a little bit, you are not really in the "Hot Seat." I need you to use your imagination with me in this section because in some cases, I will not be talking about physical sweat. Sometimes you could be sweating mentally, but other times pressure will cause you to sweat physically as well. However, what needs to be understood is that some kind of sweating will be taking place.

If the "Hot Seat" you are in does not make you at least a bit nervous, I cannot really call that a "Hot Seat." Now you may be saying, *"Everybody has their different levels of pressure to deal with, and some people may deal with pressure without sweating at all or without getting even slightly nervous."* My response to that may be surprising; however, that kind of pressure never has and will never create any Champions, nor will it ever take anyone from being ordinary to becoming extraordinary! The reason for this lies in the fact that it takes breathtaking, life-changing, ridiculous, and unthinkable pressure to develop real Champions. That light stuff will not work; that small stuff will not do it; that hint of pressure will not get you anywhere far. It is going to take the kind of pressure that comes and stretches you so far and wide that you may not even recognize yourself anymore. It is going to take the kind of pressure that tries to break your spirit, your will to fight, your sanity, and your confidence. Now, if you can encounter this kind of pressure and not sweat at all or become even slightly nervous, then I need a dose of what you have! However, for most of us regular people, this kind of pressure will cause us to cry, question God, question life, reflect deeply, ask tough questions, and bring us to a place where we have to ask ourselves, *"Should I run or do I stand?"*

    I am here to tell you that if you make the difficult decision to stand and rise to the occasion, you will respect yourself much more as well as gain the respect, confidence, and support of those around you. Nobody respects a quitter, nor can you expect people to follow one. Quitting is easy; if you want to gain support, well, get ready to sweat and show those around you that you are not a quitter, and that you are not afraid of the "Hot Seat." It is through the sweat that Champions are made. The more you have sweated, in most cases, the greater you become. There is a price to be paid to become a Champion, and if you have been wondering what that price is, well I want you to know that the amount may vary but the currency used is *sweat*. Now you can stop wondering why you are not where you thought you should be in life. If you have not paid in sweat, then why live in regret? With most Champions we see, those who we look up to who have achieved great things; we will not see the moments where they sweat. There is an old saying that goes *"never let them see you sweat,"* and I agree–you should never let them SEE IT, but do not get that confused with not sweating all together.

Real Champions

    You may not ever see real Champions sweat, but I can guarantee you they are sweating each and every day to stay in first place. This is not a one-time process, where you sweat, endure, and overcome something and now, all of sudden, you are at the top forever. It does not work like that. Real Champions know that they must continue to put in the necessary work, withstand the necessary pressures, and continue to challenge their limits daily to remain the best. The second, and I do mean the "second," a Champion feels as if they have it all together and no longer have to stretch themselves, they are going to instantly begin to fall, and their competition will pass them by. Let's take a look at boxing great Mike Tyson, for example. Most people will criticize him for his criminal behavior, and questionable decisions that he made outside of the ring, which have landed him in a negative light through the public's eye, and has been extremely difficult for him to shake. However, make no mistake about it; the man was a Champion in the ring. He was feared by many and completely unstoppable in his prime.

The pressure of growing up in poverty with no opportunities forced him to train harder than anyone else, and the thought of going back to being broke, busted, and disgusted was enough to push him into greatness. At the prime of his career, when Mike Tyson stepped in the ring, losing was not an option. His tenacity and confidence in the fact that he had trained harder than anyone else were enough to destroy any and every opponent set before him. There is something about preparation that will always ease the nerves and give you untouchable confidence while in the "Hot Seat." Mike Tyson was able to be put in the "Hot Seat" in the ring and make it look as if it was not a "Hot Seat" at all. He would destroy his opponents in a few short minutes, and some in seconds. He was beating people so easily that even he started to buy into the hype. He began to let his greatness go to his head, and that was the beginning of his downfall.

Not remaining humble and sticking to the process that got you on top in the first place is a recipe for self-sabotage. He stopped training as hard, he stopped studying the videos of his opponents, and overall, he started taking short cuts because it was said that he was the best boxer in the world, and the most feared heavyweight champion. Well, as a result, a no name at the time that went by James "Buster" Douglas achieved what has been called the biggest upset in the history of heavyweight championship fights. He knocked Mike Tyson out and took his Champion status from him. However, in my opinion, it was not really Buster Douglas who took Mike Tyson's Champion status, but Mike Tyson himself, who self-sabotaged his throne by aborting the process.

Final Thought

We can never get too comfortable while being in the "Hot Seat." As with the example with Mike Tyson, he obviously made it look easy, but that does not mean it *was* easy. After so many victories, he began to feel that being in fights was effortless to him, and he forgot that the "Hot Seat" has no favorites; it only respects those who are able to rise to the occasion. We can learn a lot from this story about staying ready. There is a saying that goes, *"If you stay ready, you will not have to get ready."* If you want to be a Champion, then you will have to remember that staying ready is a necessity. You never know when your opportunity will come for you to shine. You will never know when something unexpected will come and try to knock you off your focus. You will never know who is plotting to take your position, so that is why staying ready is so very necessary.

When you are in the "Hot Seat," it is never a pleasant feeling. You are being tried and tested, but it is important to remain calm. When you are under pressure, panic is your worst enemy. You do not want to let people see you panicking. You may not have it all together, but you need to act like it. The greatest Champions, like Mike Tyson in the ring, make things look easy, but that is only because they know how to stay calm under fire. This is a skill you will have to develop if you want to become a Champion and remain on top. If you want to lead people and gain the trust of others, they will need to see you conquer some situations that test your limits first. They will need to know, *"If I start following them, they will not quit on me when things get tough."* In closing, I will leave you with this saying from an unknown author, and it goes, *"You will never know yourself, until you see yourself under pressure."*

LAW #6

The NOW Factor

"Only put off until tomorrow what you are willing to die having left undone" Pablo Picasso

Chapter 6

LAW #6

The Now Factor

"Getting an idea should be like sitting on a pin; it should make you jump up and do something." E.L Simpson

    Time is an interesting concept, is it not? No one can stop it, slow it down, or alter it in anyway. It really amazes me how some people can live 100 years and not get as much accomplished as someone who has only been alive for 25 years. We are each given 24 hours in a day, but how many times that 24 hours will reset is out of our control. We do not know the exact date, hour, or minute that our time will expire, but one thing is for sure; the clock is ticking. As I write this book, the clock is ticking, and as you read these powerful concepts, the clock is ticking. Do me a favor; decide in your mind what it is you would like to accomplish most in your lifetime. Pause; hold it in your mind for just a second, then read this next statement aloud to yourself: *I DON'T HAVE ALL THE TIME IN THE WORLD TO GET IT DONE!*

    If you have ever struggled with procrastination, you should wake up every morning, visualize what it is you would like to accomplish, and repeat this simple statement with strong emotion. When you think about it, we actually don't have all the time in the world to accomplish our goals. You are given a certain period of time to get it done, and anything that you did not get done dies with you. How many people do you think died before their dreams were realized? How many people you think died with great ideas that could have changed the world? How many people do you think not only had their bodies buried in caskets, but also had their life changing, generation altering ideas buried with them? How many? I can imagine an unspeakable number. How many people lay on their death bed with regrets, mourning not that they are leaving the Earth, but that the opportunity to fulfill their purpose is leaving them? I imagine an unspeakable number.

So where does this leave me and you? Well, I am glad you asked, because this leads me into something else I have noticed in great Champions, and it is something I like to call the "Now Factor." There is not one single person that is considered a Champion by others that does not operate in the "Now Factor." It is undeniable, and if you want to become a Champion, you will have to operate in the "Now Factor." You may be wondering what exactly the "Now Factor" is. To break it down plainly, it is a deep sense of urgency down inside the heart of a soon-to-be Champion to go be great, and to go be great today! They wake up every day thinking about their mission, and begin to actively work towards getting closer to their goals. While everyone else is putting it off until tomorrow, next week, or New Year's, true Champion candidates are trying to get there as soon as possible.

Urgency

Have you ever had a job working for someone and your boss came by and said something similar to, *"Guys, can you please work with a sense of urgency?"* Why does the boss need to say this? The reason is that your boss is aware that if a sense of urgency is not placed on the workers, then they are probably not going to get the work done as quickly as possible. Can you honestly say if your boss did not have a timeframe for your work completion that you would be sweating and pushing yourself to get it done fast? Probably not. Another reason your boss is pushing this sense of urgency is because the longer it takes to get the work done, the more resources are lost. Your boss probably operates by the popular saying, "time is money," and when you move without a sense of urgency, money is being lost, and if you are the cause of resources being lost, you could be out of a job soon. Now, if we can understand this concept while working for someone else, why is it so hard for us to understand this concept in our daily lives?

May I ask you what do you believe to be your most valuable resource? Think about it before you answer this question. What are you most afraid of losing or wasting? Most people probably would respond to this question with money. However, although money is an important and very valuable resource, I cannot agree that it is more important than time. Time is actually the most valuable resource that a human being possesses. Why do you think most employers pay people for their time, through hourly wages, salary, etc.? The reason is that employers recognize that a person's time is the only thing that is finite to a person, and once it is spent, it can never be regained. You can make more money, but you cannot use it to buy more time. True Champions understand this very important concept, and live by it every day.

As the saying goes, *"Those who decide not to chase their dreams go to work for someone who did."* They go and work for someone who had a sense of urgency to go get the job done; someone who decided that all the pain in the world would not stop them from where they were trying to go. Someone who found value in there uniqueness and decided to act upon it immediately. Listen, I have nothing against someone having a job to take care of their financial responsibilities, but to allow your job to take up more time than you spend on chasing your dreams is a recipe for misery. A sense of urgency is necessary, because once life hits you, it is very easy to become comfortable with where you are and lose your sense of urgency.

Talkers and Walkers

The "Now Factor" always separates those who love to hear themselves talk from those who do not like to talk at all, but let their actions speak for them. I can't tell you how many extraordinarily talented people I come across every day that won't just get started and see what happens. I come across countless people who say I always wanted to write a book, I just never did; or I wrote a book, I just never put it out; or one day I am going to work on this great idea I have that's been dancing around in my head for the past five years. Listen, if it is not out of your head and at least on paper by now, with so much going on in our minds, it is probably going to get lost up there real soon. If the idea is dancing around in your head, you can almost bet your last dollar that someone else is dancing with that same idea. You must realize that the longer you take to get started, the more momentum you give to the competition to introduce it to the world first. Stop just thinking about it and go do it. The Nike slogan has become a cliché these days, but it is still extremely relevant and will always be until the end of time. We have to come to the point where we stop just watching and talking about the game and actually get in it and start playing.

The phrase that I hate to hear most is, *"someone needs to go create _____ because I am tired of having to deal with this crap,"* or the famous, *"one day, somebody is going to stand up and say something about this and things are going to change around here."* My question is, why can't that someone or somebody be you? I started my textbook website business from the problems that I dealt with as a college student paying for textbooks. I was that person that got angry and said, *"Somebody should create a website we can use to sell our textbooks to each other."* My next statement was, *"that person should be me."* If there is a problem that you see not being solved and you feel passionate about, start working on it now.

I learned something very valuable from the founder of Facebook, Mark Zuckerberg. In an interview with Startup School in 2013, he shared that when he first started Facebook, he started it because it was something he wanted to use for himself, so this is why it started at Harvard. As he continued to speak in the interview, he said something extremely profound. Mark Zuckerberg stated, *"I was really excited to offer this service for our community (Harvard), but I thought to myself, one day someone was going to build this for the world……it did not cross my mind that we would be the ones who could do it, we are just college students, what do we know about building software that hundreds of millions of people would use."* He went on to say he thought bigger companies that had better engineering, more money, and more expertise, like Microsoft, Google, or Yahoo would build something like this for the world–a valid thought, in my opinion, but what he says next is what truly grabbed my attention. As Mark continued he said, *"I spent a lot of time reflecting on why we were even able to do it, and all reasons suggest that we shouldn't have been able to do it ....these bigger companies had more resources…… but the reason I think we actually ended up being the ones doing it is because we just cared way more about it."*

I believe a lot of us abort our missions and ideas because we leave it up to someone else to do it, but it just may be that you care about it way more than any other person on the planet. Have you ever thought about that? Your desire to see it realized just may be stronger than anyone else's who has ever been born. What if Mark Zuckerberg did not act right away on his feeling that we needed a platform where we could connect with real people and keep in touch with friends and family? There would be no Facebook today, and if you are reading this and you have a Facebook page that you use on a regular basis, are you not thankful or glad that this young man did not give up on his desire to see the platform become real? I hear somebody saying, *"Oh it's just a website, not really that important to me,"* ok but why do you have the Facebook app on your phone and don't go a day without checking it. This service has reunited people with lost family members; moms and dads who have never met their kids have been united through Facebook. Beyond all the negative things that people say about Facebook, it is undeniably a valuable service that is keeping the world connected and allowing businesses to build greater relationships with their clients, customers, and fans.

What are you waiting on?

What problem can you solve that you probably care about more than anyone else? Whatever came to your mind first is what you should be working on right away! Do not hold it off another day. Think about how Mark has touched countless lives through this platform that he originally felt a company bigger and better would create. How many lives can you touch with what you are allowing to lay dormant in you? People like Mark Zuckerburg become Champions financially by stepping out on what they are passionate about, the problem that they believe they care about solving more than any other individual in the world. According to Forbes, in 2015, Mark Zuckerberg's net-worth is $34.8 billion; not bad for a college dropout who started a website in his dorm with some roommates. How much money are you missing out on by not acting now on your dreams, visions, and ideas? I realize not everybody can be Mark Zuckerberg but what I can tell you is that anybody and everybody has the opportunity to be great. However, you must be willing to put your head down, put your blinders on, and get to work right now!

Someone reading this book has a multi-million dollar idea for a business, but you keep saying, *"I just do not know where to start."* Is this you? Well if it is, you do not need to know exactly WHERE to start, but what is most important is that you get started somewhere. Someone reading this book has been told they have the talent to sing or perform music professionally, and be a great recording artist or musician. However, you keep saying to yourself that you do not have anywhere to record, or you do not have the time in your schedule to work on music. How about, *"Music do not pay the bills and bring home the meals, so it is better for me to work 40-50 hours a week helping someone else build their dream."* Is this you? If so, you need to make time for your dreams, by any means necessary. I am not saying quit your job, and by all means do not quit your day job, but what you can do is work on your dream on your off days instead of resting. You can also cut down on some of that overtime you are putting in, and instead, work on something that expresses your personality or creativity. I believe we were born to create and bring fresh ideas and concepts into the world, and if we are not doing so, we are dead already– inside, that is. Re-light that fire that probably went out after you became an adult. You need an electric shock sent to the imagination and creativity parts in your mind to get you awakened and operating at a high degree for where you are going.

Later is not PROMISED

If you are saying to yourself, *"I will get it done later,"* You are setting yourself up for failure. If you want to be a Champion, you have to completely take the word "later" out of your vocabulary. Throw that word in the fire and watch it burn, never to be seen again. Your mind has to be fully alert today, and you have to be working on that thing as if you may not see next week. The truth of the matter is, you actually are not guaranteed to see next week. Are your days consumed with working long hours for someone else and paying bills, just barely to stay afloat? If it is, I know that statement may have stung you a little bit, but that is okay because you are getting ready to gain your sense of urgency back. We were not born to just work and pay bills. If you have children, you probably think something is wrong with this statement because you are saying to yourself, *"My kids have to have food on the table and a roof over their heads."* You are absolutely right, but my question to you is when they get older, what do you plan on passing down to them? Can you pass down your job to them? Are you going to tell your kids to stop dreaming and begin to live a life of just working, doing something they hate to make sure their bills are paid? Is this really what you want for your children?

I realize these are tough questions, but Champions are warriors, and they are never afraid to be asked tough questions. If you have children, you need to realize your children look up to you. They are not going to do what mommy and daddy say do; they are going to act the way they see mommy and daddy act. If mommy and daddy are always arguing over money, or stressed out because they are working dead end jobs, the children are naturally going to pick up on these things. I was the first in my immediate family to attend a huge university, going for my four-year degree. It was very difficult having no guidance, support, or advice from my family; as a result, it took me seven years to get a four-year degree. I had to make a lot of mistakes; I had to figure out how to pay for college on my own, causing me to have to take a few semesters off. It was a brutal and grueling process that would have probably been much easier if I did not have to be the one to start the legacy. To date, I cannot think of one person in my entire family who has started their own business, not even a small snack shop or hot dog stand. I am not saying this to put my family down, because I love my family on both my mother and father's side, but I have to be honest about not having much passed down to me. I was left empty-handed to try to figure things out for myself.

That is why I decided not to wait until "later" to write and get this book published, because I know there are millions of others who probably are in the same position I just previously spoke of. If this is you, realize you do not have to leave your children empty-handed as well. They did not ask to be here, and it is your job to train them to be ready for this world. If you do not instill these Champion principles in them, there is a good chance that once they leave the comfort of mommy and daddy's nest, they are going to go into the real world and be eaten alive. In the game of life, you are either doing the playing or you are getting played. You are either winning or you are losing. You are either crushing or the one getting crushed, and you can't do both.

People are sitting back waiting for the uneducated, unmotivated person to come around so they can pull them in and suck them dry of all their time, energy, happiness, and dignity if possible. That is what happens to you if you do not have anything passed down to you. The world around you uses and abuses you, and once it has no more use for you, well, you know what happens next. Are you sure you want that to happen to your children? It could have easily happened to me had I not chosen otherwise. If you do not want this to happen to your children, well then it starts with you following your passions and dreams first, and if you are that child currently getting used and abused by society, I come to tell you a Champion is lying dormant inside of you. We must come to the understanding that most of the time, it takes tears, pain, and suffering to wake that Champion up. It takes you getting fed up with life as is, and refusing to die in those circumstances. True Champions get to a point where they say, *"enough is enough,"* and a fearless attitude emerges that causes them to do things they could have never imagined doing.

Stepping Out

I believe getting started could be one of the hardest parts of the journey to becoming a Champion, because it requires you to have to step out of where you are comfortable and into the unknown. It is not easy, but I can give you a brief story about how I did it. While sitting out of school and waiting until I could pay for my education, I started working at Wal-Mart in 2007 as a truck unloader. Within 6 months, I was promoted to a support manager position, which at the time was an hourly management position. While working at Wal-Mart, I was having a difficult time getting back in school, because it seemed as if all the money I made went to paying bills. I was working 40 hours a week from 4pm to 1am, so by the time I got home, I went to sleep and was back up getting ready for work again. I learned a great deal of leadership and communication skills during that time but I was miserable, for I felt all of my dreams had been put on hold. In 2009, Wal-Mart decided to get rid of the support manager position and introduce what was going to be considered zone managers. I had a choice: go back to a regular associate position, or go into the assistant manager program, which would allow me to be on salary and making anywhere from $50,000-$60,000 a year.

That $55,000 a year sure did sound good to a 22-year-old, knowing that most of my friends in college dreamed of graduating and finding a job that paid at least $50,000. I was faced with a dilemma, because I knew I wanted to go back to school, but that kind of money could help establish me. The other issue I had was that in being friends with a lot of assistant managers, co-managers, and store managers, I seen how miserable their lives were. Once you became salaried at Wal-Mart, 40 hours a week was a joke; salaried managers in the high traffic stores were putting in 50, 60, or 70 hours every week–with no extra pay. If I did not have a life with my 40 hours a week, I knew once I got promoted again, I would probably lose every sense of who I really was. I began to realize why a lot those managers were so mean and bossy, and seemingly envious at times, because they had probably lost themselves as well for the sake of a paycheck. I must say, you will always regret it when you take money over following your heart; you will get stung every time. Real Champions use the compass of their hearts to make decisions, but that is another topic for another book.

Continuing the story; I decided I would go back to being a regular associate; which was a painful decision. The store manager said I could work anywhere I wanted to in the store, so I chose hardware and automotive, because I figured my days would probably be easy since there was not much that went on in those departments. The first couple of weeks were cool; I would come to work, do my job within the department, and leave. It was not long before I realized people were treating me different, because it seemed to them as if I had been demoted. Managers would talk to me disrespectfully, and associates I once managed looked down on me and ridiculed me due to their perception of me being demoted. On top of that, I was bored out of my mind in that department. I would go to work every day, walking down the same aisles, straightening up the same products, seeing the same people day in and day out. After about two to three months of doing that, I was absolutely miserable every time I walked through that job's doors. I would instantly become depressed every time I went over to my department. I did not know how much more I could take before I lost my mind! I was afraid to quit, because I had rent, phone, food, gas, and all sorts of bills to keep up with, but I knew I had to do something. *(Disclaimer: This is not said to demean Wal-Mart in any way; I know people who work for the company who love their jobs and go on to have great careers within the company; it is a great company, and this is only the account of my personal experience.)*

I applied to Georgia State University that same year and began working hard to get back in school. I finally ended up getting accepted into their business program, and was set to start in a few months. I thought to myself daily, *"Maybe I will just work part time at Wal-Mart and go to school,"* but I realized my depression was getting worse so I had to get out of there. I can vividly recall walking up and down those aisles in disbelief of how that was actually my life. I would began to cry, because I felt like I had failed myself, and that I was trapped in my situation. Once I realized I was actually crying, and how hurt and defeated I felt, I told myself nothing was worth that. I prayed a very short prayer that basically asked God to give me the faith I needed to step out and believe in Him as my only source of income. Five minutes later, I walked into the manager's office and gave them my notice that I was quitting. They did everything they could to get me to stay, but I had already made up my mind.

Stepping out is not easy, and I did struggle without my job, but I also noticed I was more happy about life and I felt free! That experience happened in 2009; it is now 2015 as I write this, and I have not worked for anybody else besides myself since that day. I went back into that Wal-Mart a few weeks ago, and it shocked me to see that a lot of people still recognized me and greeted me with love. I was not there to see them, however; I was there to go back to the department where my life changed. I have to tell you, when I stepped back into that department, a lot of those old emotions came back to me, and I had to hold back the tears because if I had not stepped out on faith, who knows where my life would have been? I get very emotional when I think about this story because that day, sitting in that hardware department at a Wal-Mart in Atlanta, Georgia, I vowed to never work for anybody else again another day in my life; and here I am, six years later, still holding on to it. However; if I did not put into play the "Now Factor," like many others, I would probably still be an associate with the company to this day, and obviously never would have written this book.

If I said it has been easy, I would be lying. If I said it has been a cake walk, I would surely be saying something false. No, it has been tough, but guess what? It has brought that Champion out of me! It has brought it out of me and has prompted me to write this book that will hopefully bring that Champion out of you as well! My mother works for a great company, and she would always tell me, *"Son you should come and apply here once you graduate. I am sure you will get in and can make lots of money."* I would say, *"Sorry mom, I decided I am going to go do my own thing."* The strange thing about this is she would say this almost every time I came home to visit, and I would have to give her the same response. It was as if it did not really register to her that I was truly going to figured out how to make a living on my own. Therefore, I say to you, it will be hard to step out into greatness, and not everyone is going to understand you. Not everyone is going to agree with you, and you will not get a pat on the back from everybody. Most of the people around you want to see you doing well, as long as you are not doing better than they are. Once you start doing better than them, you are probably going to begin losing a few friends, but that's okay. Do not worry about them; you have to do what's best for you, and begin stepping out on what you know is true!

Now or Never

Have you ever felt the way I did while I worked at Wal-Mart? Are you in a similar predicament now? If you answered *yes* to either of those questions, my question to you is, *"How long do you plan to stay in it?* Will it be for a couple more months, a few more years, or when you die will you still be in it? Are you okay with dying in that predicament? Miserable at work, depressed, and totally unfulfilled in life? The last moments of the most precious gift of life spent in misery just working to stay afloat? If this is you, I challenge you to take action, and take action NOW! If you are not going to do anything to change your situation NOW, there is a good chance you will remain in that circumstance until your dying day. It is NOW or Never! Again, not everybody will be able to go and quit their job, like I did. That is part of my own personal journey and level of faith. You have to operate on your level of faith, and go after what you believe in. If you want to be a Champion in life, then you have to know that it is NOW or Never!

LAW #7

COMMITMENT

"Until one is committed, there is hesitancy, the chance to draw back, always ineffectiveness." Neil Strauss

Chapter 7

LAW #7

Committed: The Art of Finishing

"If it is important to you, you will find a way, if not you'll find an excuse." Ryan Blair

In the previous chapter, we focused on the "Now Factor," and how important it is to have a strong sense of urgency. I challenged those of you who have been procrastinating to get started right away and stop wasting time. Now, in this final chapter, I have to touch on a concept that could be more grueling and more difficult than just stepping out on faith and getting started. I know you are saying to yourself, *"Stepping out of my norm and getting started is hard enough."* I agree that it certainly is difficult to get started on a journey towards a greater destination for your life; however, Champions are not considered Champions because they started something. If you truly wish to become a Champion, you must finish what you start!

The road to success is long and frustrating. If you want to become a Champion, you must defeat whoever was in first place before you, and most people will not go down without a fight if they really care about staying in first place. Yes, the road to the top can be long, complicated, emotional, stressful, and at times painful. The good news is that it lasts but a moment; however, once you become a Champion, that achievement can never be taken away from you. It will last not only through your lifetime, but if you have achieved something extraordinarily great, people will be talking about what you did for generations and generations. Therefore, I encourage you to enjoy the journey and stick to the process. We should be just as excited about the process and journey as we are the final destination. It is important that we find enjoyment in our work, and stay excited about solving our complicated issues.

The Road

There is a saying that goes, *"The road to success is always under construction."* I also love the quote from superstar singer, Christina Aguilera, which says, *"The roughest road often leads to the top."* If you want to be a Champion, you have to understand that there is a road to be traveled; so, let's pretend you live in Michigan, and your family wants to take a trip to Florida for a vacation. You are planning the 20-hour drive from Michigan to Florida, because taking an airplane is not an option. What would you do to start the process of getting prepared? You are probably going to make sure you have a map, or some type of navigation device with accurate directions. You are definitely going to want to make sure you have money for gas, so that the vehicle does not run out of gas before you make it to your destination. You now have everything you need, and you are ready to get on the road.

You are now on the road with the family, and you all are on your way to Florida. Five hours into the drive, out of nowhere, it begins to storm and rain very badly. It is so bad that you all have to pull over for a short while, until the rain passes over. Once the storm passes, you are back on the road, just to realize this particular highway you are on is under-construction, and we all know what that means. Traffic is moving extremely slow, so your progress is significantly decreased. You find a different route on your navigation, and with the first opportunity you get to exit, you get off and begin taking a different route to the same destination. The only problem with this new route is that it has added an extra three hours to the trip. Now you are getting frustrated, because this trip is taking a lot longer than expected. However, you continue up the road when suddenly a huge semi-truck almost side swipes you, due to the truck changing lanes without looking over first. If your reflexes had not kicked in and prompted you to swerve into the emergency lane, there is a good chance that everybody in the car could have been seriously injured.

So far, you have went through a storm, ran into some construction, re-routed, which made the trip longer, and were almost hit by a huge semi-truck. After taking about 30 minutes for everyone to gather themselves at a gas station, you are now back on the road. You drive another two hours, then all of sudden you hit a pothole, and your front tire blows out! You cannot believe what is happening, or that you are having so much bad luck. Everyone in the vehicle is frustrated and tired of all these obstacles. You are determined to make it to Florida, so you go to the trunk, pull out your spare tire, and proceed to change out the tire that is blown. After about 45 minutes wasted changing the tire, your vehicle is back on the road and headed to Florida. You, the driver, are saying in your mind, *"We are not stopping again unless we absolutely have to, and we need to get to Florida as soon as possible."* You are now about four hours away from Florida, but as you drive, you notice that your gas hand is getting low, so you begin to look for an exit. Unfortunately, you have driven over 30 miles and still have yet to find an exit with a sign that indicates there is a gas station nearby. It is now dark outside, and you are getting worried because there are no gas stations in sight. All of a sudden, you feel the pedal no longer accelerating the vehicle and are forced to stop because, you guess it, you've ran out of gas.

I have a question for you–if you were in this predicament, would you call AAA to bring you some gas so you can head back home, or would you get that gas from AAA and continue towards your destination? Most of you probably said, *"Well I made it that far, I might as well continue on with the drive being so close to my destination."* I agree that most people would probably continue with the drive, but my problem is that if we can so easily realize we should continue with this drive toward the vacation destination, why do we not see it the same way in our journey in life?

You Must Drive

Most of you probably have already said to yourself, *"I am not taking a 20-hour drive anywhere; if I cannot get on the plane, I am not going."* This is interesting to me, because most people actually feel like that when it comes to accomplishing something great in their lives. They believe there should be some type of short cut or way to get there faster without traveling the hard road. If this is you, please pay attention to this next statement: if you want to be a Champion, you cannot take the plane– you must drive! There is no option for taking an airplane to success; you must take the long road. If you do decide to take the airplane, you run the risk of not having lasting success, but only a temporary measure or illusion of success.

You may be also saying to yourself, *"Most people do not experience that much trouble on a road trip; some do, but the story is a little over exaggerated."* Well, I exaggerated the vacation story for a reason. The reason is this, the vacation story may be exaggerated, but when you are on the road to success, all of those things are guaranteed to happen, along with much worse obstacles. You are definitely going to run into some construction on the road towards your dream. Oh yes, and personal storms; such as family issues, financial issues, health issues, etc. will certainly attempt to slow you down. In addition, if you do not believe someone will try to sideswipe you on the road to success, you are in for a rude awakening. People are going to talk bad about you, tell you that what you are doing is impossible, and even intentionally try to sabotage your success. Last but not least, you will most certainly run out of gas on more than one occasion. We are only human, which means we get tired and we become exhausted. Most of the time, when we run out of gas, it is an emotional and mental battle.

The gas that we use to keep us headed in the direction towards our goals is books like this, which provide us with renewed energy to keep going. It is that pat on the back of appreciation that someone gives you, to let you know they truly appreciate all your hard work. It is that prayer, it is that inspirational video, or it may just be a talk you have with yourself saying, *"I came too far to give up now!"* You have to say this to yourself, because I believe it is that point of running out of gas that makes most people give up on their dreams. They have been battered, abused, and mentally confused on their journey, and then they suddenly come to a point where they are out of gas. The problem is that on the road to success you do not have a lifeline like AAA that exists. You cannot just call someone and have them bring you a full tank of motivation to get you back on the road. It just does not happen that way. Most of the time, you have to pick yourself back up and get back on the road. You may have to rest for a while, you may have to clean up your wounds and allow them to heal for a while, but by all means get back on the road, and do not get off until you arrive at your destination.

Attitude

Not giving up is all about having a winning attitude. If you have a negative attitude every time something goes wrong, and believe me it will, you will throw up your hands in defeat. You may blame someone else for the issue, and never take responsibility for your own success. In the story about the vacation, if that group did not maintain an optimistic attitude, they would have probably turned around when they were almost sideswiped. A negative attitude would have said, *"Well, that must have been a sign that we need to just turn around; it is not meant for us to make it to Florida."* These kind of people are not meant to make it anywhere, and I guarantee you they will not make it anywhere far with that attitude. Your will to keep going during tough times has everything to do with your attitude, and the attitude of those around you. If most of your friends and family usually have a negative attitude and mindset, you are putting your dreams at a serious risk. It is extremely dangerous for dreamers to hang out with people who have negative attitudes. You may say, *"But this is my best friend; they will not do anything to harm me."* Well, they are not harming you intentionally, but their attitude and ideas can be contagious. Your friend is not harming you; instead, you are harming yourself by continuing to hang out with quitters, and people who have no strong desire to become a Champion. I must repeat, it is very dangerous for you to keep them in your circle; you can find out the easy way or the hard way–the choice is yours.

It is probably not a mystery why I saved this subject for the last chapter. It does you no good to follow all the advice previously stated in this book just to give up right at the end. If you want to be a Champion, you will have to learn to endure until the end. I think this single characteristic outweighs any great talent, intelligence, or amazing gift a person may have. I can tell you that the most talented and most gifted people in the world are not Champions. The ones that we do see become Champions are talented, but a good majority of them are not the *most* talented. No, the ones that become Champions are simply the ones who decided to put in the sweat, and endure until they made it to the top.

I noticed that I come from an extremely talented family. On both sides of my family's tree are numerous talented and gifted individuals, and I mean unbelievable, jaw-dropping talent. However, the drive and tenacity to endure the process it takes for them to become recognized for their greatness can be absent at times. I have cousins that I will gladly admit are naturally more talented than I am. What I had to work extremely hard at came easy to them. The problem is that talent can sometimes be a curse to some people. I call it the "curse of the talented." I call it a curse because some people can be so talented that they feel they do not have to work as hard as everybody else does. They feel they do not have to prepare as much as everybody else; as a result, the one who may be less talented, but came more prepared, comes out victorious because they did not take anything for granted.

Commitment

Commitment, in the dictionary, has been defined as *the state or quality of being dedicated to a cause or activity*. Another definition defines it as *an engagement or obligation that restricts freedom of action*. The dictionary says that when you are committed to something, you are restricted of action. That means you can't do everything you want to when you want to. When you are dedicated to a particular cause or activity, sometimes you will have to give up what you want to do to remain loyal to what you need to do. Synonyms for this word include *dedication, devotion, allegiance, loyalty, and faithfulness*. If you want to be a Champion, you have to be devoted; you have to be dedicated and faithful.

The problem I see with most people, which is what prompted me to write this book, is the fact that they run away from anything that requires commitment. I know this may sting a little bit, but if you think about it, the only way you can win against all odds is if you stay committed. Most people will dream about being a Champion, but will never commit to being a Champion. Most people will talk about getting their degree, but will never commit to finishing the coursework. Most people who say they want to play in the NBA will never commit to the training required to perform at such a high level.

When we spend our lives running away from everything that attempts to tie us down, we never actually get anywhere. That person will bounce from one activity to the next, one relationship to the next, one job to the next, never finding fulfillment in anything. I see this most with talented and gifted people who have an ability to be really good at almost anything, but their problem is that their multifaceted talent makes it difficult to commit, because of all the options. This is why I call it the "curse of the talented" because without commitment the gifted/talented man/women is actually cursed to mediocrity. This is certainly a great tragedy, because being committed can almost guarantee you success 100% of the time. A committed person says, *"I may not have it all together now, but I am going to keep on working on it,"* and *"I am going to keep showing up every single day until I get it right."* Commitment is what inspires persistence, and everything submits to persistence! If you want to be a Champion, you have to make the choice to be committed through the good, the bad, and the ugly. You have to be willing to ride the waves and stay on board when things are going great, or when all hell is breaking loose. If you do commit, you will, without a doubt, be crowned a Champion for life–something no one will ever be able to take from you.

Follow Through

As I wrap up this book I would like to encourage fathers who may have had a kid prematurely to stay in their child's life and follow through with their responsibility. Parents who take the responsibility of raising their children seriously are the greatest Champions on Earth, in my opinion. If you started a business, make sure you keep working on it until you start seeing the results for which you hoped for. You may have to shut down that business and start a different one, but by all means do not give up on your dream of being a business owner; continue to follow through. If you have a dream of playing sports professionally, it boils down to your will and drive to get there. If you are already over 40 years old and you think a team is going to pick you up and pay you to play, that may not be entirely realistic. If you have suffered a life-altering injury that makes it difficult for you to live a normal life, training to play professional sports may not be the best idea for you. However, if you are physically capable of being a professional athlete, I say keep working on your game until you make it, and never give up on it.

If you are a rapper, singer, or musician and wish to get into the music business, I first must say you need to have some talent, and be willing to work on your craft daily. With that being said, go and put your music out there, and do not let anyone tell you that you cannot be a platinum artist or musician, because that is just their opinion. If you started writing a book but never found the energy to complete it, I say once you are finished reading this one, do not pick up another book until you finish yours. If you need to know what steps to take to get it published, reach out to me via email and I would be glad to have that discussion with you.

Did you start high school, but dropped out while you were younger and never found the time to go back and get your diploma? Did you start college and went for a few semesters before you had your baby or had to start work full-time? Well, do not let another day go by without working towards getting your degree or diploma, because you had no business starting it if you did not plan to finish. You may have to move some things around. You may have to give up some weekends of going out. You may have turn your phone on silent so you can concentrate, but whatever you have to do, by all means FINISH WHAT YOU START! Once you go back and finish what you start, you prove to yourself first that you are not a quitter, and second, you prove to your family and friends that you will not accept quitting in your life. You break the habit of starting something and quitting when it gets too hard. You break the habit of jumping from one thing to the next without ever fully completing anything you start. You will begin to make sure you finish and reach your goal in one area before you decide to give your energy to the next, and that is what makes you a CHAMPION. When you finally follow that thing through to completion, you will be able to look in the mirror and say to yourself, "I AM CHAMPION," and you will be absolutely right!

Conclusion

In closing, I want to first thank you for reading this body of work, and I certainly hope you are able to take something away from this book that will propel you to accomplish your dreams and goals. I decided to share some very intimate moments of my life in hopes that it may relate to something you may be going through. My hope is that through my trials and through the valuable experiences I have gained during my broken times that I may pass them down to help someone avoid some of the mistakes I made. My passion is to inspire and motivate people to tap into their purpose and to provide tools and information for those hungry for growth.

In an effort to briefly recap some of the principles laid out in this reading remember that Champions know who they are, and they stay true to their identity. Champions are not interested in becoming a watered down replica of a great original. Be you, and that will be good enough; you do not need to be like anybody else. Also, while on this journey, remember to keep your mind protected from toxic ideas that seek to sabotage your success. You have to protect your mind to stay focused, because if you cannot stay focused, you cannot stay on top. Your mind is like a computer, and you get to control what comes up on the screen.

I would like to encourage you again not to run from your pain. Pain and temporary failure have brought out the greatness in some of the most successful people to ever walk this Earth. If you avoid failure and pain, you are aborting a necessary process to becoming a Champion, and trust, you will never make it to where you are trying to go. Pain and failure are necessary ingredients to success, which brings me to my next ingredient that you will not be able to avoid even if you tried. Yeah, I am speaking of the "Hot Seat." I am talking about you not shying away from pressure situations, but instead embracing them, for these situations truly expose what is inside you. Nobody is ever considered great until they are able to perform well under pressure. I remember when LeBron James first entered the NBA, and he immediately became a dominant force in the game. His first five to six years in the NBA were filled with awesome highlights, stats, and all-star appearances; however, he did not get the full respect he deserved like some of the other great ball players. Although physically and statistic wise he seemed to be headed toward being the best player to play the game, basketball critics could not fully give him that title because of his failure to perform in pressure situations. You would hear people say, *"LeBron James would be the best player in the game if he was more clutch."* In the last seconds of the game, he seemed to lose his composure and not show up for his team when needed.

It was not until he hit a few last second game winners that he began to receive more respect from basketball critics. It was not until critics and fans seen him perform great with his back against the wall that he began to get the respect he deserved from the public, and I am here to tell you that your critics feel the same way. Your followers, your supporters, your friends, and your family want to know how you perform when everything is going bad. How will you perform when all the odds are against you? Will you run or will you stand? Will you push or will you give up? So I say, do not be afraid of the pressure, for if you fail, you can always learn from it so that it will be much easier the next time around. There is something about pressure that I did not state in the chapter, but I feel compelled to state it here. The more pressure situations you are in, the easier they become to handle. They never get just completely easy, but they become somewhat easier, and you get better at keeping your composure.

You can accomplish your goals if you believe you can, but do not forget about the "Now Factor." In that chapter, I put up a quote that read, *"Only put off until tomorrow what you are willing to die having left undone,"* by Pablo Picasso. You have to sense that your time is limited, and that you are trying to get as much done in the time you have. Take a day to rest, but do not rest too long, because there is work to be done. Start working on your dreams right away, because if you keep putting them off, you just may never pick it up. Dr. Martin Luther King, Jr. called it the fierce urgency of NOW! There has to be a fierceness to your urgency if you wish to become a Champion.

Lastly, follow through until it comes true. Stay committed and do not let anything get in the way of you completing your goal. It is not starting that makes you a Champion; it is only when you follow through to completion that you are considered a Champion. Hard times will come, but you have to be ready to stick it out regardless. Michael Jordan was cut from his high school team, and Tyler Perry was homeless and lived in his car for a period of time. Both of these individuals clearly are very passionate about what they do and both are now well on their way to becoming Black Billionaires-something extremely rare in the United States. These two individuals did not give up once the times got rough. Michael Jordan and Tyler Perry are just two examples of many who have displayed unspeakable courage and toughness. I want you to know that you are tough too; you just may not know it yet because you have not been pushed past your perceived limits. You are greater and tougher than what you give yourself credit for. You read this book to completion; now you need to go out and write the story of your life, because you are a CHAMPION.

When everything starts falling apart remember to tell yourself, "*I AM CHAMPION.*" When your money is looking funny tell yourself, "*I AM Champion*". When you are sick or suffering through pains in the body don't forget to tell yourself, "*I AM Champion.*" You get to decide your attitude through times of difficulty. This book is about the seven laws of winning against all odds and I want to close by saying you will win eventually if you keep saying to yourself, "*I AM Champion, I AM Champion;*" while never ceasing to fight for what you believe in. Give these words time to sink deep inside your heart until it becomes a way of life. A life that can only be described as "Champion Living." This does not mean everything is perfect in our lives, if just means that we are willing to *fight* for everything that is not! Good luck on your journey, may God bless you!

About the Author

William E Jennings Jr was born to Deborah and William Jennings Sr. on March 2nd, 1987 at the Cook County Hospital in Chicago, Illinois. He was raised on the south side of Chicago until his family moved to Milwaukee, Wisconsin when he was about six years old. He has always held a passion for sports, music, and business. He got his competitive nature from playing basketball throughout his years in school. He graduated from Bay View High School in Milwaukee, Wisconsin and went on to get his bachelor's degree in Business Marketing from Georgia State University. While attending Georgia State University he became the Vice President of the American Marketing Association. He also became the President of the Collegiate Entrepreneurs Organization and grew the organization from 5 members to over 60 members in less than 6 months sparking excitement for entrepreneurship all over the campus.

In 2012, he was awarded the Outstanding Minority Marketing student and Marketer of the Year award for his efforts in helping to significantly grow these two organizations on Georgia State's campus and growing his business ventures. While in college he started CheckMyBookstore.com a website where college students can create virtual bookstores then buy, sell and trade textbooks within their college community. Since graduating in 2013, he has started W. Jennings Investment Group, LLC a firm that provides a wide range of financial service solutions for clients across the Midwest region while also launching CheckMyBookstore Publishing Company in 2015. I AM Champion is the first book William Jennings has written and published. His mission is to inspire and motivate as many people as possible around the world to push towards finding their true passions and callings. In the future he hopes to continue publishing books for authors who have great talents but may not have great opportunities in front of them. He also looks to get into speaking publicly on the college and professional circuits telling his unique story of winning against all odds. If you would like to contact William Jennings Jr for a speaking engagement; to inquire about his publishing company, or just to send feedback about his book you are welcome to do so. You can also visit his website to get more information about William and receive more inspirational content. Contact information is below:

William Jennings Jr

Dallas, TX

wjennings@checkmybookstore.com

404-558-6179

www.IAMWillJennings.com

www.ingramcontent.com/pod-product-compliance
Lightning Source LLC
Chambersburg PA
CBHW071312060426
42444CB00034B/1973